STRONG
— and —
COURAGEOUS

A Journey

J.K. RUSSELL

Copyright © 2018 J.K. Russell
All rights reserved
First Edition

PAGE PUBLISHING, INC.
New York, NY

First originally published by Page Publishing, Inc. 2018

ISBN 978-1-64350-797-2 (Paperback)
ISBN 978-1-64350-798-9 (Digital)

Printed in the United States of America

Thank you everyone who believed in me! But more importantly, thank you to my Father in heaven Whose guidance and direction have brought me here.

Have I not commanded you? Be strong and courageous. Do not be afraid; do not be discouraged, for the Lord your God will be with you wherever you go.

—Joshua 1:9

Accepting Christ

Have you been wondering, with everything going on in the world, when the next war will begin, where it will begin, and who will start it? Well, I don't think about it because if it's going to happen, then it's going to happen; and no amount of worrying is going to change it, nor will it change the outcome. However, with that being said, one thing that we can make sure of is where our hearts are at with Christ. Have you accepted Christ? Are you in line with Father? And the last question is this: What will Christ find you doing when He returns? See, with Him, we shouldn't worry. He's got us. He won't fail us, and He'll be there in the end. I think about those who read my daily thoughts, and I don't make the assumption that everyone is saved through Christ. It's my hope and prayer that you are, but again, it would be an assumption and not one I'm not willing to think about and move on with because I want everyone to come to Christ. I always think about certain people in the world, and I wonder if they're saved. It's never for me to judge, so I don't, but I do pray for them. If you're at that point in your life where you're tired of running and don't know how to pray about it, I'm going to help you. Say this prayer and mean it with your whole heart. Get quiet, be still, and pray: "Lord Jesus, I confess to You all of the wrong and sinful things that I have ever done in my life. I ask that You please forgive me and wash away all my sins. I accept You as my personal Lord and Savior. I ask that You come into my heart and into my life. Amen." I accepted Christ on September 11, 2001. For reasons only known to me, that is when Christ let it be known that it was time, and I asked Him to come into my heart and my life. It was the most amazingly awesome life-changing experience of my life. It's not been easy, but I know Christ lives in me. What more could anyone want? He's with me daily and loves me unconditionally. Remember, with new faith comes the time of learning "what to do next"—church, Bible study, prayer groups, Christian fellowship. If you aren't sure where to go, talk to friends and find a local church. Or go to the internet and type in the town and state you are in, and you will find many churches. The important factor is to be in one that will help you grow in your faith. Pray about it, and let the Lord lead you.

> If you declare with your mouth, "Jesus is LORD," and believe in your heart that God raised him from the dead, you will be saved. For it is with your heart that you believe and are justified, and it is with your

mouth that you profess your faith and are saved. As Scripture says, "Anyone who believes in him will never be put to shame." For there is no difference between Jew and Gentile—the same LORD is LORD of all and richly blesses all who call on him, for, "Everyone who calls on the name of the LORD will be saved. Romans 10:9–13, NIV

Therefore, do not worry about tomorrow, for tomorrow will worry about itself. Each day has enough trouble of its own. Matthew 6:34, NIV

Those who hope in the LORD will renew their strength. They will soar on wings like eagles; they will run and not grow weary, they will walk and not be faint. Isaiah 40:31, NIV

Notes and Reflections

_____

_____

_____

Prayer
Dear Heavenly Father, I thank You for hearing my prayer. I pray that with each day, my Christian walk will continue to grow and be stronger. I pray that my faith remain strong and that I am able to recognize that in any weakness, You will give me strength. I pray that my life be everything You would have it to be and more. In Jesus's name. Amen.

Christ's Light

You are the only Bible some unbelievers will ever read.
—John MacArthur

Pastor Bailey preaches/teaches us this always. We need to, on a daily basis, let our Christ light shine. When others see the Christ in us, they see Him in the way He should be seen. Don't let the "yucks" of life outshine the brilliance that is Him.

In the same way, let your light shine before others, that they may see your good deeds and glorify your Father in heaven. Matthew 5:6

Notes and Reflections
_____

_____

_____

Prayer
Dear precious Heavenly Father, I pray that I can be a vessel for You, a light that others will come to know You as their personal Savior. Let Your light shine before men in such a way that they may see Your good works and glorify Your Father Who is in heaven. I pray that You will use me in such a way that brings You honor and glory. In Jesus's name. Amen.

Smile More

> Today, give a stranger one of your smiles. It might
> be the only sunshine he sees all day.
> —Unknown

I know, for me, life is busy; and in that busyness, I'm so focused that I forget to look up and around me. It doesn't take a second to look up and smile at someone as you pass them going into the grocery store or walking on the street. Smile and say, "Hi! How are you," whether you know them or not. You never know what their life/day has been like, so be that light even if only for that moment.

> So in everything, do to others what you would have them do to
> you, for this sums up the Law and the Prophets. Matthew 7:12

Notes and Reflections

_____

_____

_____

Prayer
Dear Heavenly Father, I pray that You will help me to stop, take a deep breath, and remember what my purpose is during the busy times in my life. I pray that I never miss an opportunity to brighten someone's day by just simply smiling. A glad heart makes a cheerful face, but by sorrow of heart, the spirit is crushed. Please give me many opportunities today to make someone's day. In Jesus's name. Amen.

Alms

Real generosity is doing something nice for
someone who will never find out.
—Frank A. Clark

This is one of my favorite things to do. I enjoy doing something for someone, and them not knowing or giving a small gift and not signing the card with nothing other than "Have a great day." Even a short prayer for someone can be the greatest gift. Just remember, though, when you do these things, do not brag about it.

And let us not grow weary of doing good, for in due season we
will reap, if we do not give up. Galatians 6:9

Notes and Reflections

_____

_____

_____

Prayer
Dear Heavenly Father, thank You for all the times you have done things for me that I didn't even know You were doing. Your Word says, "Beware of practicing your righteousness before other people in order to be seen by them, for then you will have no reward from your Father who is in heaven." Lord, help me to do for others that will be a blessing to them, but to do it with a heart that doesn't want reward. Give me the opportunities every day, Lord, to do something for someone even if it is a small prayer. In Jesus's name. Amen.

Laughter

Laughter is the music of the heart.
—Unknown

Today I received several texts from a group of ladies I have come to know and love. I laughed so hard at each one. From the silliest of texts to the needing of prayer, I was thinking how blessed I am to have them in my life. We are there to pick one another up when we feel like the pieces are too many, and we are there to lighten the mood when the need arises. I encourage you to laugh and find the positive in the world. A smile and happiness in your heart are the best medicine, and the sound of laughter is the best music.

> Strength and dignity are her clothing, And she smiles at the future. Proverbs 31:25

Notes and Reflections

_____

_____

_____

Prayer
Dear Heavenly Father, thank You for those you put in my life. Thank You that even in the midst of negative situations of life, there is always something positive. I want my mouth filled with laughter and my tongue with joyful songs. In Jesus's name. Amen.

Light

Even in the darkest of times, God is still
there and His light shines brightly.
—Unknown

In the fall, I love the colors and everything beautiful that fall is, but it was a rainy dreary day; and if you know me at all, it wouldn't surprise you to know that I was just down. Through a morning of tears, I wondered where God was that day. I had stopped at the church, and when I left, the sun shone down on me through a small circle opening in the clouds, and I just stood there and felt the warmth on my face. I knew then that God hadn't left me and He was right there. So even on those days when the world seems so dark, He reminds us, in some way, that He is there. We just need to find that "light" in the midst of the darkness. God is so good!

Notes and Reflections
_____
_____
_____

Prayer
Dear Heavenly Father, thank You for never leaving me or forsaking me even when I cannot feel You near. Help me, Lord, to stop, take a breath, and look. Help me see the light when there is darkness. In Jesus's name. Amen.

Watching

As a Christian, and knowing others "watch" how we act and listen to the things we say, we need to keep our thoughts positive because those thoughts can become what we say and they can become how we act. I will be the first to say, "I really am not perfect at this." My mind can go from positive to negative in a matter of seconds, and my words and actions will show that, but I'm getting better at it one day at a time.

> What goes into someone's mouth does not defile them, but what comes out of their mouth, that is what defiles them. Matthew 15:11

Notes and Reflections

_____

_____

_____

Prayer
Dear Heavenly Father, thank You for loving me even when I am not speaking positive things. I pray that You will continue to search my heart and show me areas where I need to grow. I want to be a light for You. In Jesus's name. Amen.

God's Plan

Some days, this is easier to write than others. However, as I learn to walk daily with Father, it will get easier, and I hope will give others an uplift for their day. I used to wonder why I was here. What was God's plan for me? A few months ago, I finally felt that I was becoming the person God has wanted me to be and I'm doing what God has planned for my life. While I know I want so much more in my walk with Him and His work, my mission trip is just the beginning. Knowing this makes my heart happy. We all have a purpose, and trusting God to lead us to it will only make us stronger in our faith, and doing His will will only make us happier and more faithful.

> Trust in the Lord with all your heart, and do not lean on your own understanding. Proverbs 3:5
> For I know the plans I have for you, declares the Lord, plans for welfare and not for evil, to give you a future and a hope. Jeremiah 29:11

Notes and Reflections

_____

_____

_____

Prayer
Dear Heavenly Father, thank You for putting me outside of my box at times and for allowing me to lean on You even when I struggle to understand. I pray that You will continue to guide me and show me Your plans. I want it to be Your will and not mine. In Jesus's name. Amen.

Sisters in Christ

Last night I became part of a women's group named Sisters in Christ. This is an appropriate name as we are truly sisters in Christ. A new dear sweet friend felt God speaking to her heart about this. She did a great job last night, and the Holy Spirit was definitely moving. I know that she will do amazing things within this group in the name of Christ. A small group can be so uplifting in your walk. If you haven't joined a small group, please put that on the top of your list because we all need one another in some way, whether it be prayer and learning scripture or talking or listening. I didn't think I would ever really want to be a part of any group, but it's funny how what we want isn't what He has planned for us. I'm now in two groups and have started two of my own. God is good, and I thank Him for bringing these women into my life.

Notes and Reflections
_____
_____
_____

Prayer
Dear Heavenly Father, thank You for the ladies that I can call sisters. Thank You that I can be part of something great to grow in You together. I pray that You will bless and protect us all as we begin to learn. In Jesus's name. Amen.

Little Blessings

Babies are blessings from God, and each one has a purpose. No baby is a mistake. I think a new baby is one of the most positive happy events that can happen; no need to say more.

> For we are God's handiwork, created in Christ Jesus to do good works, which God prepared in advance for us to do. Ephesians 2:10

Notes and Reflections

_____

_____

_____

Prayer
Dear Heavenly Father, thank You for the blessing of little babies. Thank You for watching over and protecting them. I pray that we, as parents and grandparents, will train up the little ones to walk with You and to know You. There is nothing greater than to know that Your children walk in the way of truth. In Jesus's name. Amen.

Addiction

Two years ago, on the twenty-third of September, I smoked my last cigarette; and four years ago, on the fourteenth of July, I had my last drink. Neither one was fun anymore, and I grew tired of needing them. Each time I wanted to take up the habit again, one thing that helped me and gave me strength was repeating, "I can do all things through him who strengthens me" Philippians 4:13, ESV. We can all learn that He is our strength, and we need only to ask Him and He will be there. He never leaves our side and can get us through anything. If you're going through something today, remember that *you* can do *all* things with the strength of our Lord and Savior Christ Jesus.

> For everything in the world—the lust of the flesh, the lust of the eyes, and the pride of life—comes not from the Father but from the world. 1 John 2:16

Notes and Reflections

_____

_____

_____

Prayer
Dear Heavenly Father, thank You for the courage and strength to break strongholds that oftentimes keep us from walking completely with You. I know that with You, I can do all things. I pray that You will help me keep my eyes on You and not the things of the world. In Jesus's name. Amen.

Faith

Faith is taking the first step even when you
don't see the whole staircase.
—Martin Luther King Jr.

This quote was given to me as a gift yesterday. It's one of my favorites. Faith has been a struggle at times for me, as I'm sure it has been for you. But faith has brought me where I'm at today. In forty-nine days, I'll be boarding a plane to Guatemala where I'll know no one and is someplace so far out of my comfort zone. Many have wondered why I'm going. Well, let me tell you that I never once second-guessed my decision to go. I feel, with all my heart, that it is a God thing. My faith that God would use me somehow in the medical field has led me here. My faith in knowing that He will be there when I get off of the plane and through that week is enough for me. So whatever nudging you're feeling from God, take that first step. Don't be afraid because you can't see the entire picture, or staircase if you will. Just know that He has you and will take care of you and will be with you throughout your journey.

Notes and Reflections
_____
_____
_____

Prayer
Dear Heavenly Father, thank You for the Holy Spirit and the nudging that He does. I pray that when I feel the nudge, I will have the courage to say yes. I want to take that first step each time, but I need You. I can do nothing without You. Help me to know that it is from You and not my own understanding. In Jesus's name. Amen.

Blessings

As I have been scrolling on Facebook, I've noticed how many pictures there are of kids laughing, people hugging, and so much love. Everyone is blessed, each and every day, in some way. We need to take a moment and just close our eyes and think about our day. I just got home from my grandson's birthday party, and while I was watching the little ones run, play, laugh, and eat cake, I realized how blessed I truly am. I see my boys grown up and the woman each married, and again, I am truly blessed. When we are having a bad day or just a day, stop and think, "How has God blessed me today?" It may be the smallest thing or, in my case today, a huge blessing. My heart is happiest when I hear one of them say "Grandma," and I just thank God for them.

> Behold, children are a gift of the LORD, The fruit of the womb is a reward. Psalm 127:3

Notes and Reflections

_____

_____

_____

Prayer
Dear Heavenly Father, thank You for children. They truly are gift from You. I want to thank You for the blessings that You give me each moment of every day. I pray that when I am struggling, You will remind me to stop and think, You are here. In Jesus's name. Amen.

Doubt

Don't doubt in the dark, what God showed you in the light.
—Unknown

This was said to me by a coworker one day when I was questioning my purpose. "It was a God moment," she said, because she hadn't thought about that sentence in many years. She told me to believe and have faith that everything is heading in the right direction and that I had truly heard from God about it.

God shows us things when we least expect it. At least, that's how it is for me. I never expected to be on the journeys I have been on and am still on, but my faith in Him and knowing He has shown me bits and pieces of things are so exciting! Have I doubted? Absolutely! But in the midst of my doubting, God brings me a shining moment; and I realize that, once again, He has brought my purpose out of the darkness I doubted in and into the light of His promise.

Notes and Reflections

_____

_____

_____

Prayer
Dear Heavenly Father, Your ways are not my ways. Your thoughts are not my thoughts. Thank You for that. I pray that I continue in faith learning Your ways and Your thoughts. I want to be on Your journey because I know that it will bring me much joy. Please watch over and protect me as I continue on with the purpose that You have shown me. In Jesus's name. Amen.

The Future

> The best thing about the future is that it
> comes only one day at a time.
> —Abraham Lincoln (1809–1865)

I hear people talk about "tomorrow not being promised," and that's true. Only God knows how long we will be traveling through on this earth before we reach our final destination. Sometimes I think about this and wonder if I have given my today all that I can and have. I have given God my today and all of me. When I think of the future, I think about years from now, but we need to live each day as if it's our last, and that should include being in prayer, being in His Word, being a blessing to someone, etc. God doesn't give us *all* the information about our future because if that happened, where would our faith in Him go? So we live one day at a time and put our trust and faith in Him, knowing He is guiding us in everything.

> Only I can tell you the future before it even happens. Everything
> I plan will come to pass, for I do whatever I wish. Isaiah 46:10, NLT

Notes and Reflections

_____

_____

_____

Prayer
Dear precious Heavenly Father, thank You for going on before me. I pray that You will show me Your plan for my life and that You will give me the courage and strength to live it. Thank You for all that You do. In Jesus's name. Amen.

Faithful

Faith does not eliminate questions. But
faith knows where to take them.
—Elisabeth Elliot

I think that faith brings so many questions even though it really shouldn't. But at the same time, it's what helps our faith to grow. When we have questions about life, spiritual gifts, scripture, a calling on our heart, etc., we need to remember to not try to answer the questions ourselves. We need to take them to our Father in heaven. Only He knows the answers, and while He isn't going to give us *all* the answers (like we would like), He will guide us into seeing and hearing what He wants us to. I've questioned so many things, especially over the past ten years, but I feel that through prayer and meditation, I'm beginning to see some answers. Have I liked all of them? No, but He loves me and knows what's best for me, and so I accept them. Being an RN without a license has weighed heavily on my heart, but He has shown me that even without that license, I'm still able to go and help others in the medical field (which is my heart). He answers questions and prayers in His time and for His glory. So take your questions to Him. Be patient for an answer, and in the meantime, remain faithful to Him.

Guard my life, for I am faithful to you; save your servant who trusts in you. You are my God. Psalm 86:2, NIV

Notes and Reflections

_____

_____

_____

Prayer

Dear Heavenly Father, thank You that even when I ask why, You still are faithful to answer. I pray that when Your ways or thoughts are not mine, I will be faithful to You. You know me so much better than I do. I trust You. In Jesus's name. Amen.

Facebook

This morning I was reading some things on Facebook, and one thing that sticks in my mind is that I read, "God is watching you read this, so don't scroll without liking this post," and few other posts like that. First of all, God doesn't concern Himself with whether or not we "like" a post on Facebook. What He *does* care about is whether or not we are reading His Word, sharing our faith, praying, being faithful, and being the kind of Christian that shines for others our light of Christ. As Pastor Bailey has taught us in preaching the Word, teaching the Word, and living the Word, that's what Father cares about. Don't make Facebook more than it is. Get your Bible out and read it. Like it, love it, get out there, and share it with others.

> Your word is a lamp to my feet and a light to my path. Psalm 119:105, ESV
>
> And He said to them, "Go into all the world and preach the gospel to all creation. He who has believed and has been baptized shall be saved; but he who has disbelieved shall be condemned. Mark 16:15–16

Notes and Reflections

_____

_____

_____

Prayer
Dear Heavenly Father, thank You for your Word. I pray that social media will not consume me. I pray that I will not be more concerned with liking a post today that a friend shares, but instead I will be reading a post that You shared so many years ago. In Jesus's name. Amen.

Life's Surprises

Over the weekend, I was thrown a surprise birthday party. I was blessed as there were family and close friends that came to celebrate this time with me. This morning I was thinking about being surprised and how heaven will look. I know that probably doesn't make sense to think of the two together. But we've grown up hearing and being taught that the streets are made of gold and jewels adorn, but what if we were given a glimpse of heaven now? How would that spoil any surprise of how heaven will look when we get there? We picture it in our minds of how beautiful and glorious it will be, but we can't truly know. In Revelation, scripture tells us, but I know it will be better and more spectacular than where my mind goes with it. So for now, we can imagine and know we will one day be surprised. For myself, that is all I need for now.

> Then the angel showed me the river of the water of life, bright as crystal, flowing from the throne of God and of the Lamb through the middle of the street of the city; also, on either side of the river, the tree of life with its twelve kinds of fruit, yielding its fruit each month. The leaves of the tree were for the healing of the nations. No longer will there be anything accursed, but the throne of God and of the Lamb will be in it, and his servants will worship him. They will see his face, and his name will be on their foreheads. And night will be no more. They will need no light of lamp or sun, for the Lord God will be their light, and they will reign forever and ever. Revelation 22:1–5

Notes and Reflections

_____

_____

_____

Prayer

Dear Heavenly Father, thank You for the glimpses of heaven You give us while we are here on earth. Thank You that You don't reveal everything to me so that I can be surprised once I get to heaven. What a glorious day that will be. I pray that You will help me to see those little things each day and to make the most of them. In Jesus's name. Amen.

Day to Day

God gives you 86,400 seconds in a day. How many of those have you used to say "thank you"? When beginning prayer or even your day, do you begin with praise and thank-you's? You should, I should, and we all should. Beginning the day, thanking God for all that He has done and all the many blessings should be something we do—not out of "habit," but because He has given us His *all*—so we should thank Him. I thank Him for His grace and forgiveness. I praise Him for who He is in my life and will always be. Sometimes we get so busy with day-to-day activities (life) we forget who gave us this life and the time in it. So today, take time to say, "Thank You, Lord, for . . ." You'll find that each day, you'll find yourself thanking Him more and more.

> Giving thanks always and for everything to God the Father in the name of our Lord Jesus Christ. Ephesians 5:20
>
> Give thanks in all circumstances; for this is God's will for you in Christ Jesus. 1 Thessalonians 5:18

Notes and Reflections

_____

_____

_____

Prayer

Dear Heavenly Father, thank You for being my rock, my comforter, and my everything. I pray that even when circumstances come that are less than desirable, I will remember to thank You. Thank You, Lord, for the 86,400 seconds you give me to say thank you. In Jesus's name. Amen.

Passions

One of my favorite nursing school instructors once said to me, "I would hate for you to miss an opportunity because you didn't go after your passion." Passions—we all have them. Some are smaller than others, but they're still passions. It's what we do with them that matters. If you have allowed them to go from a burning blaze to a small smoldering flicker, then you need to pray about it. Ask Father to ignite in you that fierce blaze that used to be there. When working on your passion, remember to do it unto Him, Who put it in your heart before you got here.

> Whatever you do, work heartily, as for the Lord and not for men. Colossians 3:23
>
> I will instruct you and teach you in the way you should go; I will counsel you with my eye upon you. Psalm 32:8

Notes and Reflections

_____

_____

_____

Prayer
Dear Heavenly Father, thank You that You put in my heart a passion. Thank You that you instruct and teach me the way I should go. I pray that the fire I have for You will be more than a smolder and will not only ignite me but also those around me. In Jesus's name. Amen.

Yes, Lord

> We gain strength, and courage, and confidence by each experience in which we really stop to look fear in the face . . . we must do that which we think we cannot.
> —Eleanor Roosevelt

This quote . . .

At times, the Lord calls us to do things that possibly scare us, but in the midst of what we're doing, we gain strength in Him and courage and confidence in knowing He is with us and He allows us to see that with Him, we can do anything. So instead of thinking, "Wow, I really can't do that," say, "Yes, Lord, and amen." There are many things He calls us to do that we balk at because we think we aren't good enough, strong enough, or our faith isn't where we feel it should be, but God's got this. He's got us. He wouldn't call us into something that would harm us. So the next time you feel like God is calling you into something that is a bit scary, just remember, He is with you.

> I can do all things through Christ which strengthens me. Philippians 4:13
>
> For God hath not given us the spirit of fear; but of power, and of love, and of a sound mind. 2 Timothy 1:7
>
> Casting all your care upon him; for he careth for you. 1 Peter 5:7

Notes and Reflections

_____

_____

_____

Prayer

Dear Heavenly Father, thank You that in Jesus, I can do all things. I pray that You will give me courage and strength to say yes when You say go. Thank You that I am able to cast all of my cares upon You and You will care for it all. In Jesus's name. Amen.

Hearing Him

In the past couple of days, I haven't written anything. It's not that I don't want to, but some days I just don't know where to go with this and what Father would have me to share. It's really like life. We know what we want to do, but we don't know how to get there. We want to share things about the Lord or just our thoughts but aren't sure where Father would take us with it, so we just don't say anything at all. It's during these times we need Him more than ever for guidance and direction and for the words that just don't come without His help. He is always there. We just need only to pray and ask.

>Your word is a lamp to my feet And a light to my path. Psalm 119:105
>
>I will instruct you and teach you in the way you should go; I will counsel you with my eye upon you. Psalms 32:8

Notes and Reflections

___

___

___

Prayer
Dear Heavenly Father, thank You that even when I can't hear You, You are there. I pray that You will show me what You are wanting me to learn and guiding me where I should go. I want to hear You. I pray that You will help me to quiet myself to be able to hear You. In Jesus's name. Amen.

Letting It Go

How many times have we heard that? We struggle with letting the hurtful things go that have happened in our life. With letting it go comes forgiveness. Father says in Matthew 6:14–15, "For if you forgive other people when they sin against you, your heavenly Father will also forgive you. But if you do not forgive others their sins, your Father will not forgive your sins." It's not always easy to do. I'll be honest. Last year, I finally forgave the one person I hadn't been able to forgive. But by the grace of God, I did. I feel that in my life, I've forgiven everyone who has hurt me in some way. When we hold grudges, we only hurt ourselves because that person you're angry with doesn't care and chances are that person probably doesn't remember or think they've done wrong. Grudges take so much energy and so much time. Don't give in and allow them to control you. Today make that decision to forgive. Do we forget? Absolutely not, but moving on can only strengthen your relationship with God. That grudge won't still be a barrier between you and Him. You'll be able to give Him your *all*! He will renew you and refresh you. Trust Him.

    Therefore, if anyone is in Christ, the new creation has come: The old has gone, the new is here! 2 Corinthians 5:17

    Trust in the Lord with all your heart, and do not lean on your own understanding. In all your ways acknowledge him, and he will make straight your paths. Proverbs 3:5–6

Notes and Reflections

_____

_____

_____

Prayer
Dear Heavenly Father, thank You that I can trust in You to help me to forgive those who have hurt me or done wrong against me. I want my relationship with You to be all it can be, and I pray that each and every day, You help me to remember that. I pray that You will show me if I have not fully forgiven so that I can grow in You. In Jesus's name. Amen.

Kneel

> I have been driven many times to my knees by the overwhelming conviction that I had nowhere else to go.
> —Abraham Lincoln

I have a plaque in my home that says, "When life gets too hard to stand . . . kneel." When we get overwhelmed with life's circumstances, what do you do? I get mad, cry, shut down, and shut everyone out, including God. We sometimes feel that no one can understand what we're going through. We feel, while it's huge to us, "Would God think it's trivial?" We spend time hurting when if we would just simply talk to our Father, our hurts would heal, our hearts would be mended, and our faith would be stronger. Don't make going to God a "last resort." He should be our first and only. He *wants* to be our protector, and He *will* take care of our needs. But also, during our prayers of asking, make them a prayer of praise and thanksgiving.

> Is anyone among you suffering? Let him pray. Is anyone cheerful? Let him sing praise. Is anyone among you sick? Let him call for the elders of the church, and let them pray over him, anointing him with oil in the name of the Lord. James 5:13–14
>
> Ask, and it will be given to you; seek, and you will find; knock, and it will be opened to you. Matthew 7:7

Notes and Reflections

_____

_____

_____

Prayer

Dear Heavenly Father, thank You that I can ask, seek, and knock anytime, anywhere. I pray that in times when life is going great or it seems too much to handle, I will always come to You. I pray that I don't shut You out. You are my strength and comforter. In Jesus's name. Amen.

The War Room

Today, I watched *War Room*. If you haven't seen it, it's an amazing movie about the power of prayer, forgiveness, and obedience to God. My prayer life is anything but passionate right now. I know in my heart that I want more. God is waiting to hear from me, and I know this. Where are you at in your prayer time? Do you have a time you set aside for prayer? Do you pray throughout the day? Do you pray for certain people or all people? Our country? The world? God speaks to us through the Bible. Christians speak to God through prayer. Prayer is such an important part of a Christian's life; prayer can be in song or in words.

> I give thanks to my God always for you because of the grace of God that was given you in Christ Jesus. 1 Corinthians 1:4
> Pray without ceasing. 1 Thessalonians 5:17
> For everyone who calls on the name of the Lord will be saved. Romans 10:13

Notes and Reflections

_____

_____

_____

Prayer
Dear Heavenly Father, thank You for Your grace. Thank You that I have a portal between heaven and earth. I pray that as life gets busy, I will continue to set aside time for You. I pray that as things come up during the day, I will turn to You. Thank You that there are movies that remind us how easy coming to You really is. In Jesus's name. Amen.

Unconditional Love

This morning, on my way to work, I was listening to WCIC. I've heard others say that at the right moment, for the things going on in their life, there will be a song that just makes you think, "Wow! Thank You, God. I needed to hear those words." Today was that day for me. The name of the song was "Never Too Far Gone" by Jordan Feliz, and one part of it says, "You will never outrun my love. / There's no distance too far, that I can't reach you. / There's no place that's so dark, that I can't find you. / Anywhere that you are, if you need proof. / Take a look at these scars, and know I love you." I think so many times that I've thought, "How can God possibly still love me after?" It restricts my time with God in prayer, meditation, and being in the Word. But when I heard that song this morning, I was so convicted in that knowing no matter what, He's got me. He's always there for me and is just a prayer away. So remember, even in the midst of our darkest days, He is always right there and He loves us, no matter what.

> So we have come to know and to believe the love that God has for us. God is love, and whoever abides in love abides in God, and God abides in him. 1 John 4:16
>
> But God shows his love for us in that while we were still sinners, Christ died for us. Romans 5:8
>
> Who shall separate us from the love of Christ? Shall trouble or hardship or persecution or famine or nakedness or danger or sword? Romans 8:35

Notes and Reflections

___

___

___

Prayer

Dear Heavenly Father, thank You that You are love. Thank You that You can use a song to remind me of that. I pray that in my darkest times, I will remember that You got me. I pray that You will use me to help someone else. In Jesus's name. Amen.

God's Love

We all want to be loved, to have that unconditional—even with the good, the bad, and the ugly days—kind of love, the kind of love that means no matter what, that person is and always will be there for you and will give you grace in the midst of your ugliness. We have that in Christ Jesus. On days when we feel that nothing is going right, our attitudes are anything *but* Christlike, and we just want to cover our heads with the blanket and stay in bed. He loves us unconditionally, and His grace is amazing. While Christ wants us to have a great day, He also knows we aren't perfect and that we need to feel His love, to feel His peace wash over us, and when we ask Him, He is so happy to give us that and more. Sometimes we don't feel loved, but that's when we need to look to Him, pray, and know that He does love us and always will.

>But God shows his love for us in that while we were still sinners, Christ died for us. Romans 5:8
>
>Three times I pleaded with the Lord about this, that it should leave me. But he said to me, "My grace is sufficient for you, for my power is made perfect in weakness." Therefore I will boast all the more gladly of my weaknesses, so that the power of Christ may rest upon me. 2 Corinthians 12:8–9

Notes and Reflections

_____

_____

_____

Prayer
Dear Heavenly Father, thank You that Your grace is sufficient for me. I pray that when I don't feel loved, I will turn to You in prayer. I pray that when my attitude is ugly, I will feel Your peace. I pray that I can learn to love the way that You do. In Jesus's name. Amen.

Being Fed

I hear people talking about being "fed" in their faith. I never really understood what that meant, but I'm learning. I work with some pretty great ladies, and they are fed by the Holy Spirit in different ways. One is fed during vacation Bible school, and one is fed through music. Both are fed by the same God but in such unique ways. It's important for our souls to be fed because if we aren't, then our faith remains as it is; and while that's not a bad thing, we need that "feeding" to feel refreshed and sustained. We need to feed our spirit by being in God's Word, spending time in prayer, meditation, etc. I know, for me, it's all that; and when I don't get to do those things because, let's face it, I allow life to get in the way, I feel drained and in a desert. Don't let life drag you down and keep you from allowing the Lord to refresh you. Be in His Word daily even if just for fifteen minutes. You'll be amazed what He can do in such a short period of time.

> The spirit of man is the lamp of the Lord, searching all his innermost parts. Proverbs 20:27, ESV
>
> And he who searches hearts knows what is the mind of the Spirit, because the Spirit intercedes for the saints according to the will of God. Romans 8:27, ESV

Notes and Reflections

_____

_____

_____

Prayer
Dear Heavenly Father, thank You for Your Word. Thank You that we can all be fed even in different ways. I pray that You will search my heart and show me what I need to learn. Thank You for all that You do for me. In Jesus's name. Amen.

Sermon Points to Ponder

One Monday, I was talking to my friend, Dave, and he had shared with me something he had taken away from the sermon the Sunday before. I sat there and said, "I didn't hear that." He went on to explain why he understood it the way he had, and I added my thoughts. It was then I wondered, "How many took notes?" So today during church, I was looking around, and I noticed a fair amount of people taking notes. Some were writing in the bulletin, some had notebooks, and some were using their iPad. I take notes, and I post them on our church's FB page in the Sermon Points to Ponder group. I started that group because everyone takes something different away from the sermon, and I wanted to share my notes and read others, if they so choose to share them. Notes are a good way to remember what was taught on Sunday. You are able to go back, reflect, and read scripture about the sermon. So if you're wondering if you should be taking notes because you might miss something "key," I think that would give you the opportunity to talk with others about it, share your thoughts, and it would give you the opportunity to talk about our God, His faithfulness, and His love for us.

> Consequently, faith comes from hearing the message, and the message is heard through the word about Christ. Romans 10:17

Notes and Reflections

_____

_____

_____

Prayer
Dear Heavenly Father, thank You that you give each of us what we need in ways that apply to just us. I pray that I will continue to search and listen for what You are telling me each time I hear the Word preached. In Jesus's name. Amen.

His Eyes

I've posted several times the video for "What a Wonderful World" by Louis Armstrong. It's one of my most favorite songs ever! It makes me smile and think about all of God's creations and how wonderfully beautiful everything is in this world.

> I see skies of blue and clouds of white
> The bright blessed day, the dark sacred night
> And I think to myself what a wonderful world
> The colors of the rainbow so pretty in the sky
> Are also on the faces of people going by
> I see friends shaking hands saying how do you do
> They're really saying I love you

When the ugliness of the world rears its head, I think of our Father and how much He loves me. If I would just take a look at the world and pray that I see things through His eyes, it can be so amazing. The world is a beautiful place. If you are having a "blue" kind of day, ask Him to allow you to see things through His eyes, and you'll see beauty like you've never seen before.

> Lift up your eyes on high and see: who created these? He who brings out their host by number, calling them all by name, by the greatness of his might, and because he is strong in power not one is missing. Isaiah 40:26

Notes and Reflections

_____

_____

_____

Prayer

Dear Heavenly Father, thank You for all the beauty around me. I pray that even on dark days, I will see the world as You made it. I pray that Your power will shine down. Thank You for the music that warms our heart and makes us think about You. In Jesus's name. Amen.

Relationship

It's not who you are that holds you back;
it's who you think you're not.
—Unknown

In order to learn more about who you are and gain a deeper understanding, you need to develop a relationship with God. He will reveal even more of who you are and your purpose as you seek Him through His holy Word. If you are willing to take the blinders off and truly see yourself as you were created to be, I invite you to take the time and look at yourself through the eyes of God. His eyes are truly the window to your soul.

Notes and Reflections

_____

_____

_____

Prayer
Dear Heavenly Father, thank You for Your Word and that I can develop a relationship with You. But the Lord said to Samuel, "Do not look on his appearance or on the height of his stature because I have rejected him. For the Lord sees not as man sees: man looks on the outward appearance, but the Lord looks on the heart." I pray that You shine a light on every corner of my heart and show me who I am. I can look in a mirror and see who I am on the outside, but I want to grow closer to You, and by that, I need to know who I am in You. In Jesus's name. Amen.

Disappointments

This morning I was disappointed and a little heartbroken by something that happened, and I'm not going to lie—I cried a little. However, I couldn't allow that disappointment to linger, yet how often do we allow our disappointments in life to keep us from having a great day? When these things happen, it's so important to give it to our Father, which I did. I'm allowing Him to handle it for me so I can move on and have a better day. You can do the same. Allow Him to fill you with peace and love. God never promised us perfect days, but He has promised us a life everlasting, an eternity without heartache and disappointment.

> Do not be anxious about anything, but in everything by prayer and supplication with thanksgiving let your requests be made known to God. And the peace of God, which surpasses all understanding, will guard your hearts and your minds in Christ Jesus. Philippians 4:6–7
>
> And we know that for those who love God all things work together for good, for those who are called according to his purpose. Romans 8:28

Notes and Reflections

_____

_____

_____

Prayer
Dear Heavenly Father, thank You for Your peace and love. Thank You for Your promises to me. I pray that when disappointments come, I will lean on You and I will give it all to You. I pray that Your peace will guard my heart and my mind. In Jesus's name. Amen.

Don't Look Back

I've come too far to look back. There's a song about that. In fact, that's the title. When I think about where I've been and where I'm at now, I think, "Wow, God has really changed my life," and it's all good because that's what He does. He took my life and has made it into something more beautiful than I could have ever imagined. He can *and* will do that with your life if you let Him. He wants to and He's waiting on you to turn it over to Him. Pastor Bailey preaches and teaches us on a regular basis to let go of our past. We've come too far to look back. Give Him your past, give Him your present, and give Him your future. He's got it!

> But Jesus beheld [them], and said unto them, With men this is impossible; but with God all things are possible. Matthew 19:26
>
> Therefore if any man [be] in Christ, [he is] a new creature: old things are passed away; behold, all things are become new. 2 Corinthians 5:17

Notes and Reflections

_____

_____

_____

Prayer
Dear Heavenly Father, thank You for taking me from where I was to, where I am now, and where I am going. I say yes and amen to You. I pray that others will come to know You because of the work You did in my life. Thank You that old things passed away and all things became new. In Jesus's name. Amen.

Raindrops

Alone we are a single raindrop but together we are the rain.
—Unknown

I love this. I saw it on the shirts of a JFL team today. It inspired me because it was the "logo" for a kid's team, and I thought, "If they get it, why can't adults?" God didn't design us to do things alone. But in that, He wants us to do things *with* and *for* Him. Think of the things we could do together with our Father. World peace is at the top of my list. Just imagine everyone coming together in this world and loving one another, becoming that torrential downpour of rain (love). That's the kind of world I want to live in. It may be a childish wish/dream, but it has become part of my daily prayer. You can begin to make a difference toward being that first drop of rain. Be that person that says, "Hi" or "How are you?" or just helps a neighbor out or even someone you *don't* know. It's never too late to be a raindrop.

A new commandment I give unto you, That ye love one another;
as I have loved you, that ye also love one another. John 13:34

Notes and Reflections
_____
_____
_____

Prayer
Dear Heavenly Father, thank You for showing me love that I may love another. I pray that we will become united and love one another and have peace that can only come from You. I pray that I will be the first raindrop and that others will follow. In Jesus's name. Amen.

Attitudes

> The remarkable thing is, we have a choice everyday
> regarding the attitude we will embrace for that day.
> —Chuck Swindoll

I had a chance on Sunday to choose my attitude. Something had happened, and when I talked to Dave about it, he asked, "Did you allow your being a child of God to shine?" I thought about it for a moment and said, "Yes." It was at that moment I realized how God has changed my life. The old me would have used a few choice words and would have been so mad. But this new me, I like her. She was calm; she wasn't upset; and never once did she yell. Now, I don't tell you this to brag on myself, not at all. I'm telling you this because in life, stuff happens and it's up to us on how we act. Do we let our Christ light shine? Or do we let the darkness come through? Our attitude is a choice. That saying "What would Jesus do" comes to mind, and He would have shown grace and forgiveness. In our daily walks, we need to strive to be like Him. Our hearts and, yes, our attitudes need to reflect our love for Him. We need to think before we speak.

> My dear brothers and sisters, take note of this: Everyone should
> be quick to listen, slow to speak and slow to become angry. James 1:19

Notes and Reflections

_____

_____

_____

Prayer
Dear Heavenly Father, thank You for the free will to make our own decisions. I pray that my heart and my attitude would be Christlike. I pray that I would be slow to speak and slow to anger as situations arise. In Jesus's name. Amen.

Prayers

Without prayer we don't have a prayer.
—Unknown

Prayer is so important to our spiritual life and walk. Right now, with the presidential election right around the corner, it's vitally important. But more than that, when do you pray? Do you pray during the good and the bad? I know we are pretty constant when life is handing us lemons to be on our knees praying, but when things are going well in our lives, do we pray praises? Do you spend time in prayer to start your day? Throughout your day? To end your day? Father wants to hear from us, and without prayer, how do we get through life? When we don't pray, how can we expect things to change? I get that sometimes we just feel defeated and wonder why pray because things won't change anyway. But that's when we should pray the most and the hardest. Father answers our prayers in His time. Or sometimes, we should be thankful He *didn't* answer a prayer. He knows best and what is going to help us and not harm us. So "when life gives you more than you can stand, kneel." Father is right there waiting.

Pray without ceasing. 1 Thessalonians 5:17

Notes and Reflections

_____

_____

_____   _____

Prayer
Dear Heavenly Father, thank You that I can come to You with anything anytime. Thank You that I don't have to be anxious about anything. I pray that I will take the time to say "Thank You" when life is good and pray that I will say "Change me" when times are not. In Jesus's name. Amen.

Self-Help

Have you ever looked at a part of your life and wondered about how you were going to fix it? You agonize over what to do, how to do it, etc. Then you get out your computer and start looking things up on Google or Bing because, you know, you can find the answer to anything on the internet and because it's there, then it must be true, right? Well, that might be the case for some things, but what about finding answers to our life with Father? Our "how-to" books are numerous, but do you get out the one book that has the answer or explanation for virtually everything in your life? It has answers on love, money, adoption, etc. If you look in the back of your Bible, there are sections that have the topic and then the scripture you need to reference. So before you go into cyberworld to look for the answers, pick up your Bible and read. I promise you that everything in that one book is the absolute truth. There's no wondering. It was spoken by God, so how can it be wrong?

> But from there you will seek the LORD your God, and you will find Him if you search for Him with all your heart and all your soul. Deuteronomy 4:29
>
> You will seek Me and find Me when you search for Me with all your heart. Jeremiah 29:13

Notes and Reflections

_____

_____

_____

Prayer
Dear Heavenly Father, Lord, as I try to play the "fixer" of my life, may I be reminded of Your goodness and faithfulness in everything. I pray, Lord, that my faith remain strong during the times of trial in my life. Thank You for giving me the only how-to book I need. In Jesus's name. Amen.

Stress

Have you ever woken up and thought, "I have so much to do today, but I'm not going to stress out," only to find yourself stressing out? This is before I ever got out of bed. I know I'm not the only one that this happens to if you're being honest. Instead of praying before getting up, I found myself up and in the midst of the chaos that was my day. How do you handle days like this? When life gets hectic, chaotic, stressful, etc., what we do or don't do can have a great impact on our day. I should have prayed before getting up and just given Father all my worries about getting things done, this trip, etc. Father wants to hear from us no matter what. Talk to Him, give Him your day, and ask Him to change it to make it His day. Allow Him to take over your thoughts and attitude. Your day will be so much better and flow so smoothly. Trust Him.

> Peace I leave with you; my peace I give you. I do not give to you as the world gives. Do not let your hearts be troubled and do not be afraid. John 14:27
>
> Do not conform to the pattern of this world, but be transformed by the renewing of your mind. Then you will be able to test and approve what God's will is—his good, pleasing and perfect will. Romans 12:2

Notes and Reflections

_____

_____

_____

Prayer
Dear Heavenly Father, thank You for reminding me that this is the day that You have made. I will be glad and rejoice in it. Lord, I pray that as life happens, You will renew my mind and give me Your peace. I pray that I will not stress out and that I will trust completely in You. In Jesus's name. Amen.

Salvation

> Do all the good you can. By all the means you can. In all the ways you can. In all the places you can. At all the times you can. To all the people you can. As long as ever you can.
> —John Wesley

I've heard many people say to me that they know they're going to heaven because they're a good person and they do good things. Well, it says in Romans 10:9, "If you declare with your mouth, 'Jesus is Lord,' and believe in your heart that God raised him from the dead, you will be saved." Yes, Father watches what we do, and He sees how we act, but that's not what saves us. However, as a child of God, being good is something we should strive for on a daily basis. Our actions *scream* about our walk with Christ. Be that person who wakes up in the morning and starts their day with Christ, and then begin doing the good works of the Lord. It can be something simple. It's up to you.

Notes and Reflections

_____

_____

_____

Prayer
Dear Heavenly Father, thank You for saving me the day I asked You to come into my heart. It is a day that I will never forget. I know that I am going to heaven, but I just pray that as I continue through my day, I will do the works of You so that maybe another can come to know You as their savior and the assurance of their eternal home. In Jesus's name. Amen.

One by One

> We are blessed in so many ways; many things we take for granted
> but we should stop and be thankful each and every day.
> —Catherine Pulsifer

I take things for granted. We all do if we're honest. Each day is a gift from Father, and many blessings are shown to us. How we treat each day and accept His blessings is up to us. Sometimes a blessing is right in front of us; and because we're too busy being upset or negative, we miss out on His goodness. One blessing I want to share is the blessing of where I work now. Instead of looking at the twenty-minute drive (especially in the winter), I look at it as I have twenty minutes to listen to praise and worship music to start my day. I don't take for granted my coworkers, and I'm thankful and I'm blessed to be working in a place that prays before a staff meeting and encourages me to spread my wings in all that I do. Yes, I make mistakes, but they aren't dwelt upon, and one last blessing is that my coworkers are Christians, and that has allowed me to grow in my faith and how I perceive things that are going on. I could write more, but you get the idea. There's a song titled "Count Your Blessings": "Count your blessings, name them one by one. / Count your blessings and see what God hath done." So, count your blessings and don't take for granted your life and the things and people in it.

> Giving thanks always and for everything to God the Father in
> the name of our Lord Jesus Christ. Ephesians 5:20

Notes and Reflections

_____

_____

_____

Prayer

Dear Heavenly Father, thank You for opportunities You give us to grow in You. Thank You for my job and my coworkers. I pray that You bless them as they have blessed me so much. I pray that I will not take for granted where You have me and the people You have in my life, not just at my job. In Jesus's name. Amen.

God's Knocking

This morning, I was thinking about the picture of Jesus standing at the door, knocking. Have you seen it? It's one of my favorites. I remember being asked, "If Jesus was at your door, would you let Him in, and what would you say to Him?" I would, without a doubt, let Him in. I would offer Him something to eat and drink. I would allow Him to rest if He needed and would be patient while being full of questions, even knowing He wouldn't tell me everything because if He did, where would my faith be after that? Think about this: Why wait for Him to knock on *our* door? Go to Him. Seek Him out. He's there waiting to open the door for *us*. He's waiting for us to ask Him questions and to be faithfully fed. I know I don't seek Him as much as I want to and need to, but I'm trying to change that. I have several things on my plate right now, and I'm learning to trust Him in each one. It's not always easy because I want an immediate answer, but an answer will come. Open the door. Let Him in. He's waiting.

> I know your deeds Behold, I have put before you an open door which no one can shut, because you have a little power, and have kept My word, and have not denied My name. Revelation 3:80
>
> Be like men who are waiting for their master when he returns from the wedding feast, so that they may immediately open the door to him when he comes and knocks. Luke 12:36

Notes and Reflections

_____

_____

_____

Prayer
Dear Heavenly Father, thank You that all I have to do is knock to meet with You. I pray that I will search You first in everything. Thank You for the inspiring pictures to remind us how simple it is. In Jesus's name. Amen.

Trust

> I know God will not give me anything I can't handle.
> I just wish he didn't trust me so much.
> —Mother Teresa

How many times have we said that? I'm guessing many many times and probably not every day, but we have at one time or another. I don't believe that Father just deliberately gives us "issues" to deal with, but in every situation of our lives, He gives us the opportunity to go to Him with what's going on and to trust Him by turning it over to Him. In more ways than we can imagine, He will be there for us. We may not see it right away, and we might even ask, "Why?" I oftentimes wonder if He gets frustrated with me, shakes His head, and thinks to himself, "Why doesn't she come to me?" Father loves us, and He doesn't like it when we struggle. But I feel like He just wishes we would trust Him more. And in doing so, we would begin to feel that weight lift and we would see that the things we are trying to handle, He is already handling for us.

> I can do all things through Christ who strengthens me.
> Philippians 4:13

Notes and Reflections

_____

_____

_____

Prayer
Dear Heavenly Father, thank You for trusting me with so much. I pray that You help me to understand and to deal with it in a Christlike way. I can do all things through You Who strengthens me. I pray that I will remember that and that others will see You in me. In Jesus's name. Amen.

Broken

God can heal a broken heart, but He has to have all the pieces.
—Author Unknown

Lately, I've had friends lose loved ones. Those loved ones aren't just in human form. Some have four little legs, and they give you an unconditional love that just warms your heart. Grief has stages. No matter your loss, you'll go through each one. But remember, during the process, to include Father. Allow Him to help you get through it. But remember you have to give Him *all* the pieces of your broken heart, no matter how many. Father can help you put them back together. Each day is a new one, and with each day, your heart will mend. You don't forget, but the memories you hold will last a lifetime. When my mom got sick and I helped take care of my Grandma Ruth, she and I would talk in the evenings. I never tired of listening to her stories about growing up during the depression and when her and Grandpa got married, just so many stories. I felt closer to her than I had ever felt. When she passed, my heart broke. I didn't realize my heart could hurt that much again. It had broken before into pieces I never thought would heal. But when I prayed about each loss and gave each piece to Him, slowly I could feel peace again. He gave me back my heart and the memories I will hold on to forever.

> For everything there is a season, and a time for every matter under heaven: a time to be born, and a time to die; a time to plant, and a time to pluck up what is planted; a time to kill, and a time to heal; a time to break down, and a time to build up; a time to weep, and a time to laugh; a time to mourn, and a time to dance. Ecclesiastes 3:1–4

Notes and Reflections

_____

_____

_____

Prayer
Dear Heavenly Father, thank You for mending my broken heart when I give You all the pieces. For everything, there is a season. I pray that I will remember that the next time my heart breaks. I pray that I will remember that my strength comes from You. In Jesus's name. Amen.

Spiritual Gifts

> What you are is God's gift to you, what
> you become is your gift to God.
> —Hans Urs von Balthasar, Prayer

God gives us all a spiritual gift or gifts. Did you ever take a class to find out what yours are? I did, and my gifts were teaching and service. When I first became a member of FBC, out of nowhere, I said I would teach the high school–aged kids. I say "out of nowhere," but God knew what He was doing. Those few years I taught were wonderful, and I miss the ones I had in class. But I can say that not only did I teach them but I learned from each and every one of them. Service is where I'm at now. However, I've incorporated teaching with service. While on my mission trip, I was able to serve our Lord by helping in the clinic and teaching a mother in labor the correct breathing technique to help with the pains. Both gifts have been amazing. You have a gift or gifts. Find out what they are by praying about it and taking a class that has that as its focus. When we use our gifts, we give back to Him. We serve Him by using them, and in my mind, He smiles about it. And remember the one great and glorious gift He has given us is eternal life with Him.

> As each has received a gift, use it to serve one another, as good
> stewards of God's varied grace. 1 Peter 4:10

Notes and Reflections

_____

_____

_____

Prayer

Dear Heavenly Father, thank You for my spiritual gifts. I pray that I will use them for You and to serve others. You're an amazing God that has blessed my life so abundantly. Thank You for what I have done and what I am going to be doing. I pray for Your guidance and direction as I continue on this path. In Jesus's name. Amen.

Giving

When you care enough to lift a spirit, you can change the world.
—Hallmark

When was the last time you saw someone down and said an encouraging word or just simply smiled at them? I know I've talked about it before, but with the holiday season coming up, it's even more important. It's that time of year when we're busy decorating, having dinners together, buying gifts, and wanting/wishing for things that aren't really important. I've seen the faces of people who just want that friendly smile because they matter, or you could even buy them a cup of coffee—nothing like a cup of hot coffee on a cold morning. The thing is, in the hustle and bustle of the Christmas season, take the time to invite someone to the Christmas Eve service or even the Christmas Day service and, even crazier, your home on Christmas Day for dinner. I know it's our thinking in this day and age, and yes, we want to be cautious, but it's uplifting to be in the midst of praising God or in the midst of the kids playing and the smell of dinner cooking. So that one invitation, that one cup of coffee, that one, anything, can change someone's world. Father wants us to help others. He wants us to be uplifting to others.

> This is my commandment, that you love one another as I have loved you. John 15:12

Notes and Reflections

_____

_____

_____

Prayer
Dear Heavenly Father, thank You for the spirit of power and love. I pray that I will be the person that makes someone's day. I pray that when You nudge me to do something, I will say yes. I know personally what a blessing that is to have someone do something for me, even if it is just a cup of coffee. In Jesus's name. Amen.

Lesson

Today I'm learning about growth, thankfulness, and having faith in Father. These are all lessons on a daily basis, but what do we truly get from them, and do we feel that we have the right? I don't know about you, but I sometimes feel that I don't because there are people out there in worse shape than I. This week has been rough as I have the bug going around, my new car decided to give me issues today, and I forgot to put an announcement in the bulletin. So here's what I've learned from this week: Lessons are tough because we think, "Ugh! Seriously?" Well, think about this: How can getting upset change what is going on? It can't, and I was reminded of this, by Father, as I was working this morning. He has calmed my spirit, and I can feel the peace of His love. It's going to work out because I know He has this, and I no longer need to worry about it. If you are feeling overwhelmed today, give it to Him. He's got you, and He's got this.

> Take my yoke upon you. Let me teach you, because I am humble and gentle at heart, and you will find rest for your souls. For my yoke is easy to bear, and the burden I give you is light. Matthew 11:29–30

Notes and Reflections

_____

_____

_____

Prayer
Dear Heavenly Father, thank You for the new lessons we learn every day. I pray that with each one comes a new perspective in my walk with You and that I can show others the love of Christ in me. In Jesus's name. Amen.

Say Yes before You Regret It Because You Didn't

Today I'm going to visit a dear friend in the nursing home. I cared for her when I worked in home health, but I've known her for many years. I have said, since I saw her last year at Christmas, that I would make more of an effort to go see her before something happens, but I haven't. That's what happens, isn't it? We say one thing, yet we do another, or rather don't, and then it's too late. Spending time with her won't take a great big part of my day, and I do miss her. So think about this: Has your time spent with Father been pushed by the wayside? Do you tell yourself that I'll spend time with Him later? Yet "later" never comes and your days turn into weeks and then into months and so on? And before you know it, it's too late. Don't let that happen. Don't let your time with Him be pushed aside by other things. Make that time. Set aside that time. I'll admit, I'm guilty of this. Not weeks, but days can go by, and I'll say just a little prayer here and there, but what I really am missing is quality time spent with Him. He wants us to spend time with Him, talking to Him, listening to Him, and reading His Word. It shouldn't be a "when I get time." It should be an "I've set aside this time in the morning/evening." Unplug from the world, and make this His time. I promise you that you won't regret it.

> But when you pray, go into your room and shut the door and pray to your Father who is in secret. And your Father who sees in secret will reward you. Matthew 6:6

Notes and Reflections

_____

_____

_____

Prayer

Dear Heavenly Father, thank You for the nudge we receive when it comes to needing to be in Your Word and in spending time with You. I thank You for not condemning us when we don't make time like we should to spend with You, and I thank You for always being there when we do make that time. I thank You for not turning away from us. In Jesus's name. Amen.

Seasons Change, Father Never Does

This morning, as I sit here watching the snow fall, I started thinking about how our lives are like the seasons and how we can compare the seasons to what Father is doing in our lives.

- Winter—He's clearing out the old, dead stuff in our lives to prepare for
- Spring—where He's preparing to grow something wonderful in our lives to prepare for
- Summer—where He's giving us our time to be alive with all of the new He grew in us and for us to grow in Him, and then
- Fall—as He's preparing to clear out what is bogging down our lives.

I have many things that need to be cleared out and thrown out to make way for all the new He is doing in my life. I always say that when it rains in the spring, He is washing everything clean, and then I'll see a new very green blade of grass poking its way through the last of winter. It's amazing. He can do that for you too, you know. Talk to Him as your "winter" is here. Ask Him to help you figure out what needs to be cleared out to make way for new growth in Him.

> As for man, his days are like grass; As a flower of the field, so he flourishes. When the wind has passed over it, it is no more, And its place acknowledges it no longer. Psalm 103:15–16

Notes and Reflections

_____

_____

_____

Prayer
Dear Heavenly Father, I thank You, Lord, for never changing and being the constant in my life. I pray, Lord, that I allow the changes You want to make in my life for each season of my life because I know that without You, I can't make those changes. I pray I am able to see each change and give You all praise and glory. In Jesus's name. Amen.

The Mirror

When you look in the mirror, what or who do you see? Do you see the person you want to be? Do you see the person God made you to be? I remember a time in my life when I stopped and actually looked in the mirror. I literally didn't recognize the person looking back at me. Who was she? Who was she supposed to be? Was this who I was made to be? It was in that moment I decided to make a change. I left that life and never looked back. It's been eleven years this October, and I can finally look in the mirror and recognize the person looking back at me. Am I one-hundred-percent healed from my past life? No, but I'm becoming more of the person God created me to be day by day. He is slowly putting me back together, and while I know I'll never be perfect by any means, with Christ in my life, I know my life will be His. God is patient, and He makes changes in us—sometimes overnight but most times it takes a while. But God is patient. What would we do without His patience with us? It's during the times of change in our lives that He's creating in us the person He's always known us to be for Him. Take a moment to look in the mirror. Who do you see?

> As in water face reflects face, So the heart of man reflects man.
> Proverbs 27:19

Notes and Reflections

_____

_____

_____

Prayer
Dear Heavenly Father, thank You for the face in the mirror. You remind us daily that we are Yours and that You created each of us for a purpose. Thank You for being patient and for the wonderful changes You have made and are making in my life. In Jesus's name. Amen.

Heaven

I've been listening to a new song, and it talks about the war in me, but in the end, He will be victorious over all. From the shadows and the grave, we'll be brought into the light and into His love. How beautiful is that and will be because Father wants us all to be on the receiving end of His love for us? Don't be afraid to give Him your war, your battle, and your fight. He fights our battles, and He is always victorious. I think about my war and about dying but only in the sense of Him winning and what being taken into heaven will be like. I know we can't begin to get it, but in my mind (a child's mind), there will be a huge gate with angels all around with my grandparents there and others who have gone before me ready to walk me through. On the other side is Jesus with arms open. So there, the battle will be over. Give your battle to Him, and get ready for Him to be victorious over it. Don't allow the battle inside you to keep you from the rewards He has, waiting for you here and in heaven.

> Enter through the narrow gate. For wide is the gate and broad is the road that leads to destruction, and many enter through it. But small is the gate and narrow the road that leads to life, and only a few find it. Watch out for false prophets. They come to you in sheep's clothing, but inwardly they are ferocious wolves. Matthew 7:13–15

Notes and Reflections

_____

_____

_____

Prayer
Dear Heavenly Father, death is something that is inevitable, and while some don't truly know You and know that heaven is real, I thank You for giving me the childlike thought of how entering into heaven and what heaven will be like. I pray, Lord, that You give me the words to speak to others about Your greatness and a life of eternity with You. In Jesus's name. Amen.

Unconditional Love

Today I'm reminded that being a tiny human comes with an unspoken amount of trust from those caring for them. They trust you to feed them, play with them, read to them, care for them, and just be there for them. I have two in my care today, and I love them unconditionally, and they know they can count on me for whatever they need but not necessarily what they want. Isn't our relationship with Father like that? We trust Him to care for us, to always be there for us, and to love us unconditionally. He sees to all of our needs, and as far as our wants, it depends. If our want isn't the best thing for us, then He really doesn't bother Himself with it. However, I believe that if our want is something that can bring Him praise and glory, then maybe not right away, but in His time. He will see that want is given to us, and you better believe it will be way more than we could have thought of, and there will be a blessing somewhere in there.

> Trust in the Lord with all your heart and lean not on your own understanding; in all your ways submit to him, and he will make your paths straight. Proverbs 3:5–6
>
> Commit to the Lord whatever you do, and he will establish your plans. Proverbs 16:3

Notes and Reflections

_____

_____

_____

Prayer
Dear Heavenly Father, today I'm reminded that no matter our age, we all need to feel cared for and to be able to trust those we're with at any given time. Thank You for allowing me to know that I can now and always trust You and know that You love me unconditionally. I pray, Lord, that I can continue to show others the love that You have. May Your light shine through me to others. In Jesus's name. Amen.

World Peace

I listen to the news (sometimes) and read the *New York Times* (when it pops up on my phone), and what I'm reading is so disturbing that my heart breaks for others. Sometimes, even though we know He is there, we may wonder where God is during the mess of this world. Does it make sense that things should happen if He is there? Not at all, but God didn't do this to the world; man did. People have a tendency to blame our Father, but the truth of the matter is, there is so much hate in this world that this is the result. So, my friends, instead of getting all up in arms over what we can't control, get all up in what we can do, and that is prayer and pray for one another. These are times when people and countries need prayer and Jesus more than ever, including our own. Don't let the hate of the world seep into your life. Pray for not only those you know, like, and love but for the enemy. Believe it or not, they need our prayers and love the most. In my prayers, I pray for world peace. You might think it's out of reach for that prayer to be answered, but in my heart of hearts, I know one day there will be peace worldwide, and it will be because of Him. That makes my heart happy.

> But I say to you, love your enemies and pray for those who persecute you. Matthew 5:44
>
> Bless those who curse you, pray for those who mistreat you. Luke 6:28

Notes and Reflections

_____

_____

_____

Prayer
Dear Heavenly Father, thank You for the peace You give me in my heart as I pray for the world. I pray for those who haven't found or felt Your peace, and I pray that they learn to turn to You for everything. In Jesus's name. Amen.

Broken

Yesterday during church, I heard Pastor Bailey say, "It doesn't matter how broken you are; God can fix it. We matter to God, and He is our comforter." That one sentence made me think all day about my life. When I finally began my journey with Father, even while going to church, I thought there was no way I could be fixed. I was damaged, broken, angry, and really had given up on being happy. But then something happened. God not only brought several people into my life, but I finally had a sense of peace and my walk with Him became stronger. So you see, it doesn't matter what we've been through in life, God was, is, and has always been there (although we wonder) and has a plan to fix our brokenness. We just need to talk to Him and allow Him to work in our life. Not all situations are the same, so I believe He customizes His plan for us, and we should have no worries about whether or not it will work because it's His plan, not our own. Our own plan never truly works. Trust Him. Talk to Him. Allow Him to fix what's broken in your life. There will be tears of anger and upset during the process, but He will turn them into tears of joy and happiness, and you'll build a solid foundation of faith and trust in Him because, you see, we all need Jesus.

> My flesh and my heart may fail, but God is the strength of my heart and my portion forever. Psalms 73:26
>
> Fear not, for I am with you; be not dismayed, for I am your God; I will strengthen you, I will help you, I will uphold you with my righteous right hand. Isaiah 41:10

Notes and Reflections

___

___

___

Prayer

Dear Heavenly Father, thank You for fixing what has been so broken in me and my life for so long. I know that with You, I can do anything, and I know that You are the only one that can fix what is broken. Thank You for picking up the pieces of my life and making me whole again. In Jesus's name. Amen.

Friendships

We all have had that friend who says, "I'm always here for you." At the time, we believe that they will in fact be there. However, more times than not, that friend is there for you on their schedule, unfortunately. However, there is one who will always be there for you. He will always be there for you when it seems that no one else will be. Father is there 24-7, 365 days a year. All we have to do is ask. Actually, He is there even when we don't ask or forget to ask. He wants us to talk to Him about everything, about it all. There is nothing too big or too small for our God. He is there for you. Sometimes I'll be doing dishes or just sitting, looking out the window, and I'll just strike up a conversation with Father. In the midst of my chattering (I chatter a lot)—it never fails—He shows up. I can feel His presence, and I can hear Him speak to me. What a friend we have in Him.

> Keep your lives free from the love of money and be content with what you have, because God has said, "Never will I leave you; never will I forsake you." Hebrews 13:5
>
> Come near to God and he will come near to you. Wash your hands, you sinners, and purify your hearts, you double-minded. James 4:8

Notes and Reflections

_____

_____

_____

Prayer
Dear Heavenly Father, I thank You for always being there in every time of need that we may have in life. You are an unfailing God, and Your presence is always felt. Help me to be that person in someone's life that can be there for whatever they are needing in that moment. Teach me to be a witness to them and have the ability to pray for their needs. In Jesus's name. Amen.

Serenity Prayer

God grant me the serenity to accept the things
I cannot change; courage to change the things I
can; and wisdom to know the difference.
Living one day at a time; enjoying one moment at a time
accepting hardships as the pathway to peace; taking, as
He did, this sinful world as it is, not as I would have it;
trusting that He will make all things right if I surrender
to His Will; that I may be reasonably happy in this life
and supremely happy with Him forever in the next.
Amen.
—Reinhold Niebuhr (1892–1971)

This prayer is one that is used a great deal for addiction. But it doesn't have to be used just for that. I use it from time to time when I've reached my limit on life and have forgotten to whom I need to take my frustrations daily. It gives me peace of mind and soul.

Surrendering to His will has been a difficult thing at times for me, but it doesn't need to be. It should be the easiest thing ever. I know, for me, I'll be saying it every morning and throughout the day. And I will do this without fail because if I don't come to the realization that I can't change it, only He can, then I'm going to miss out on some pretty wonderful things in life. Don't miss out. Allow Him to "grant you the serenity."

Notes and Reflections

_____

_____

_____

Prayer

Dear Heavenly Father, You give us strength in the midst of our storms, and You give us what we need to get through them. Thank You, Lord, for allowing me to trust You in all circumstances of life. In Jesus's name. Amen.

The Movie

God has you. Remembering this and keeping our faith walk strong are sometimes difficult especially when things in our lives aren't going as we had hoped. We pray and talk to Father, but sometimes our prayers' answers don't come quick enough. We live in a society of impatience and demand. We want things when we want them and get frustrated and discouraged when they don't happen in our time. But remember, He gives us what we need, and He will get us through even the darkest points of our lives. Don't give up. Don't quit praying. Don't quit talking to Father. Even in the midst of our frustration and ugliness, He is there and He knows. He knows what you want and need. I love the Hallmark channel (who doesn't?), and as I'm watching the movies, I think, "Really?" Life isn't like this at all. But you know what? Life *can* be like that, only in a different way. In the movies, everything always turns out beautiful and loving because they found true love. Well, with Father, it's a love that's more pure and true than any movie can portray. Our lives will never be a movie, but we can have a stronger faith and a beautiful loving relationship with Him. He loves us.

> Give thanks to the God of heaven, for his steadfast love endures forever. Psalm 136:26

Notes and Reflections

_____

_____

_____

Prayer
Dear Heavenly Father, thank You for the movie that is my life. It has had many ups and downs, and I know that You have been there through each and every one. I pray that I remember to give You all praise and glory for the good and the bad because without You, my movie would have had a different ending. In Jesus's name. Amen.

The Unknown

Sometimes in life, things are thrown our way, and we don't get it. We wonder, "Why? Why did it happen? Why me?" But the one thing we can always count on during those times is Father. We can count on Him to go ahead of us, to equip those that we will need, and to help them be prepared, and He is there to give us peace with the understanding that He is God and all things are known to Him. I have a friend who is facing an unknown. She accepted Christ, and while she believes He's got this, she's still scared. I think it's hard not to be scared when life throws us an issue. But remembering Who can get us through it is everything. He is our strength and our peace; He is our everything. The next time life throws you an unknown (and it will), remember Who is in charge; remember Who has got you and your situation; and remember Who loves you so much that He has gone before you. Trust in Him.

> Trust in the Lord with all your heart and lean not on your own understanding; in all your ways submit to him, and he will make your paths straight. Proverbs 3:5–6

Notes and Reflections

_____

_____

_____

Prayer
Dear Heavenly Father, thank You for being the one constant in the unknown of life. I pray that others see You as the one in charge of everything. Let me remember that in the midst of my unknown, You love me and are with me and that You won't leave me. I pray that I continue to put my trust in You and You alone. In Jesus's name. Amen.

Amazing God

I'm not sure how to make this one make sense, so I'll start at the beginning. I'm trying to physically prepare myself for my next mission trip, and part of that is walking because that's how I travel when I get there. So this evening, I was looking at the sky and trying to decide if I should chance it and go walk. The sky was blue with quite a few angry-looking clouds hanging out, but beyond that, there were beautiful fluffy white clouds. I always used to look at the clouds and think that each one took on a different shape.

Anyway, I decided it would be worth the chance of getting rained on because it was just so nice out. There was such a cool breeze, and I thought, "Thank you, God." About halfway into my walk, my ankles and shins began to hurt, and I thought, "No, this isn't going to happen because these are the right shoes, and I have to be ready." So I began praying. Isn't He amazing? Not only did He make my walk very pleasant, but the pain left me. I had the best walk I've had since I began a few weeks ago, and I smiled the whole time. He can do this for you too, you know. He's always there, waiting for us to come to Him, to allow Him to make the way clear for us. Talk to Him. Allow Him into whatever you're doing. He wants to take that walk with you, go for a drive with you, sit on a park bench with you, etc.

> For God is working in you, giving you the desire and the power to do what pleases him. Philippians 2:13, NLT

Notes and Reflections

_____

_____

_____

Prayer

Dear Heavenly Father, thank You for always going before me and preparing the way. You have equipped me with everything I need to do the work of Your kingdom. When I think I can't do it, You gently remind me that I can and that You have me in all circumstances and situations. Thank You for giving me a pain-free walk and for allowing me to prepare to journey again to a place that I can help others in Your name. In Jesus's name. Amen.

Our Destination

We're only here traveling through this land. Our final destination is to be with Father in the kingdom of God. I pray that as we prepare for the New Year, our hearts are with Him, our thoughts are on Him, and we continue to live for Him. Some days, I find this difficult because, well, I'm human. I make mistakes. But because of His mercy and grace, I know I'm forgiven. See, He doesn't expect us to be perfect. I think He does want us, though, to strive to be more Christlike in our hearts, thoughts, and the way we live. So when that day comes that we reach our destination and we are there to meet Him face-to-face, He will say, "Well done, my child." That's what I want for you as well as myself. So let's start the new year strong in Him. I'm starting a new devotional book, and I can color the pages. (Yes, I'm still a child at heart.) I'm excited about it. I also have one to start after this one is done, so I'm preparing. You can too.

> Therefore, if anyone is in Christ, he is a new creation; old things have passed away; behold, all things have become new. 2 Corinthians 5:17
>
> Yet those who wait for the LORD will gain new strength; they will mount up with wings like eagles, they will run and not get tired, they will walk and not become weary. Isaiah 40:31

Notes and Reflections

_____

_____

_____

Prayer
Dear Heavenly Father, as we move through this life, awaiting our final destination, I thank You for knowing I'm not perfect, but thank You for allowing me to know that Your love for me is most perfect. I ask for the tools in preparing myself for my final destination and that I might use those tools to show others of Your love and forgiveness. In Jesus's name. Amen.

God's Creations and Me

God loves each of us as if there were only one of us
—Augustine

How amazing is that? God is so big that not only He loves us all but He loves us like we are His only child. However, sometimes there are days when we wonder if God has taken a leave from us and moved on to someone else. But the thing is, God never leaves us. He is always with us. Our lives will have many trials and tribulations, but God is there with us through each and every situation. He doesn't leave us, ever. He watches over us, and even when we do things that aren't right, He is still with us. Remember this: God created the universe and everything in it. So with that in mind, remember why He created us. He created us to love us and so that we may have eternal life with Him so He can continue to love us.

> But you, O Lord, are a God merciful and gracious, slow to anger and abounding in steadfast love and faithfulness. Psalm 86:15
>
> See what kind of love the Father has given to us, that we should be called children of God; and so we are. The reason why the world does not know us is that it did not know him. 1 John 3:1

Notes and Reflections

___

___

___

Prayer

Dear Heavenly Father, thank You for loving me. Thank You for allowing me to know that You're there through everything going on in our lives. Thank You for Your creation of everything in this world that is beautiful and for loving me. I know sometimes I feel like You've left me, Lord, but I know in my heart You haven't, and it is I who has turned away from You. Thank You for never giving up on me and continuing to love me every day. In Jesus's name. Amen.

The Good News

A few years ago, I read an article that helped me make the decision to quit reading the newspaper and watching the news, not because I don't want to know what's going on in the world but because I simply couldn't take the negative and horrific things that were being reported. So what about this? What if only positive things were reported? Just one day, only positive and uplifting things? How about this headline: "This Is The Day That the Lord Has Made; Let Us Rejoice and Be Glad in It"? Then go on to say, "The flowers are blooming, the sun is shining, the birds are singing, etc."? What a wonderful paper or newscast. You know, the Bible is the most positive writing we have in this world today. It was spoken to others by God, and it's full of His love and promises to us. Reading this book is the only "news" I need. It's uplifting and full of the gospel truth. So if you haven't yet, pick up a copy and start reading. You won't be disappointed or disheartened. You'll be in awe at the love of our God.

> Now, O Lord GOD, You are God, and Your words are truth, and You have promised this good thing to Your servant. 2 Samuel 7:28
>
> O give thanks to the LORD, for He is good; For His loving kindness is everlasting. 1 Chronicles 16:34

Notes and Reflections

_____

_____

_____

Prayer
Dear Heavenly Father, I know that the news, good or bad, is a daily edition. I pray for a day of peace and joy in You. I thank You for Your Word and for the truth and joy I have found in it. In Jesus's name. Amen.

Checking In

Checking in with God before we start our day is something that we should do daily. When we wake up, before we leave our beds, we should say good morning to Father. It's only right. He *did* wake us up. We should thank Him for that and give Him our day. Sometimes I think, "Well, He knows my heart, so even though I don't know what to say (especially at 6:00 a.m.), He knows already." So I pray the Lord's Prayer. And while I'm saying this prayer to Him, I pray it with all my heart because in that moment, it's just He and I. Take time in the morning to talk to Father and check in with Him before your feet hit the floor. Show your day who's got your back and is in charge. You won't regret it.

> But the Lord is faithful. He will establish you and guard you against the evil one. 2 Thessalonians 3:3
>
> Fear not, for I am with you; be not dismayed, for I am your God; I will strengthen you, I will help you, I will uphold you with my righteous right hand. Isaiah 41:10

Notes and Reflections

_____

_____

_____

Prayer
Dear Heavenly Father, thank You for waking me this morning and for allowing me a few moments with You before rising. Thank You for allowing time for just You and me. I pray that You guide my steps today, and I pray that I may continue to be in constant thoughtful prayer with You. In Jesus's name. Amen.

The Point

Is there always a point to life? Just because we don't see the point doesn't mean there isn't one. It's taking the time to reflect and allowing the point to be shown to you in one way or another. I sometimes say, "What's your point?" or "What's the point?" Well, I think that we aren't always supposed to know the point, at least not right away. Points are made when we aren't thinking about them. At least for me, that's when it happens. I'll hear something and think, "What's the point?" Then a day or two later, it'll hit me. Aah, that's the point (I can be a little slow at times on getting things). Just remember this: If we're patient, keep our faith in Him, spend time in prayer, and learn to listen, then the "points" might be revealed. Don't be disappointed though if they aren't. They will be in time, His time.

> The unfolding of Your words gives light; It gives understanding to the simple. Psalm 119:130
>
> Concerning him we have much to say, and it is hard to explain, since you have become dull of hearing. Hebrews 5:11
>
> Until I come, give attention to the public reading of Scripture, to exhortation and teaching. 1 Timothy 4:13

Notes and Reflections

_____

_____

_____

Prayer
Dear Heavenly Father, I thank You for the points that You have revealed to me. I know that right now, I won't know every point to what's going on, but one day, I'll be closer to knowing. I thank You for showing me when I least expected it, and I thank You for Your perfect timing. In Jesus's name. Amen.

Words

We use words for everything—yes, in speaking to one another but also in describing something or expressing an emotion or prayer. There are many use for words. One thing we have to remember, though, is that words can also hurt. I see (hear) this quite often as words are not said in kind. They are yelled or screamed, and oftentimes, profanity is used. This way of using words is harmful instead of helpful. Christ would never speak to us in this manner. His words are loving. His words are kind. His words are helpful, and He wouldn't approve of anyone using His name in vain. So remember, the next time you start to speak, make sure your words are correct and that they are Christlike. Think about whether or not they would be pleasing to Father. You can't take them back once they're out there.

> Let no corrupting talk come out of your mouths, but only such as is good for building up, as fits the occasion, that it may give grace to those who hear. Ephesians 4:29
>
> But what comes out of the mouth proceeds from the heart, and this defiles a person. Matthew 15:18

Notes and Reflections

_____

_____

_____

Prayer
Dear Heavenly Father, please forgive me for the words I use at times that don't bring You glory. I pray that I'm able to stop and think before using words that could hurt others. I thank You for always using words of kindness when speaking to me and words to love me, guide me, and direct me. In Jesus's name. Amen.

Tattoos

A young girl today said, "If the words you speak were tattooed on your body, would you still be beautiful?" Wow! Such a powerful thought for such a young lady. But really, think about it. What was the last thing you said or anything you have said today? If you *had* to tattoo that on your body, what would it say about you? Would it say you are a beautiful person? A man/woman of God? I know, for me, today after an amazing day worshiping God with several wonderful ladies. However, my words when I got home would not have been words I would have wanted tattooed on my body. They weren't words that someone would have said, "Now that's a woman of God." So here's the thing. Before we (I) speak, remember they need to be words that, if someone tattooed them on your (my) body, would be words that are pleasing to Father.

> Let the words of my mouth and the meditation of my heart be acceptable in your sight, O Lord, my rock and my redeemer. Psalm 19:14

Notes and Reflections
_____

_____

_____

Prayer
Dear Heavenly Father, I often think about the words I speak and whether or not they would be beautiful if actually written where others could see them. Lord, I ask that You be with the little one who spoke that sentence today. Be with her, and I pray that she continuously grows in her faith with You. In Jesus's name. Amen.

Assignments from God

I've felt lately that God gives us assignments in life. Some of those assignments can be in the form of a job, a friend—short-term, long-term, or not really specific—but you just feel you are doing what you are doing because God put you there. I feel like I have several assignments going on that God has given me and the reason being, I wouldn't have come up with these things on my own. I also don't feel like He gives me more to do than what He thinks I can do. Some assignments I feel I have completed and He has allowed me to move on, but some I'm still on assignment with, and some are a once-a-year assignment. I love knowing He has something new and exciting for me to do. Don't get me wrong; it's not all daisies and sunshine, because you see, sometimes my assignments deal with the downside of life. But with each one He gives me, I'm in constant contact with Him through prayer. He gives me the tools I need for each one, and guess what. He is always right there with me. What assignments do you feel God has placed on your heart? Are you keeping in constant contact with Him about them? Remember, He has put you there, and He will give you what you need for each one.

In the same way that you gave me a mission in the world, I give them a mission in the world. John 17:18, MSG

He says, "It is too small a thing for you to be my servant to restore the tribes of Jacob and bring back those of Israel I have kept. I will also make you a light for the Gentiles, that my salvation may reach to the ends of the earth." Isaiah 49:6, NIV

Notes and Reflections

___

___

___

Prayer

Dear Heavenly Father, I know You put things before us, and I thank You for each and every one because I know there are lessons in them. I pray that I'm able to see what You are teaching me and using it daily. In Jesus's name. Amen.

Life's Problems

I've often wondered why I have problems with one or two particular areas of my life, and I heard a comment the other day and realized, "Oh, that's why." The comment was made that Satan knows our weaknesses, and he strategically goes to work and works nonstop at trying to strengthen those weaknesses. So we have to make a choice. Are we going to allow him to continue? Or are we going to pray nonstop and show him how mighty our God is, and with God on our side, nothing will bring us down? When we get up in the morning, we need to put on our armor of God and pray about our day. Father is there, waiting to hear from us and for us to give Him our day, our weaknesses, and ourselves. But remember in the midst of this, praise Him for everything. Praise Him for allowing you to feel peace when Satan is at work. Father loves us, and we need to remember that He is mightier.

> I can do all this through him who gives me strength. Philippians 4:13
> Finally, be strong in the Lord and in his mighty power. Ephesians 6:10

Notes and Reflections

_____

_____

_____

Prayer
Dear Heavenly Father, thank You for taking my weaknesses and replacing them with strength. I know that with You, I am able to do anything and I am able to withstand anything this world throws my way. I give You all praise and glory for all that You do and for all that You are in my life. In Jesus's name. Amen.

Quiet Time

Quiet time with Father can be difficult to achieve on some days. Think about this: There are days/nights when we have difficulty falling asleep or waking up in the middle of the night. There are times when we are stopped by an occurrence (like a sudden rain). I've always believed that when these things happen, it's because Father wants to talk or He's wanting us to just listen. But let's be honest. Do we take advantage of that time with Him? I know, for me, I often make myself fall back to sleep because I'm tired or I will make a run for the car instead of spending that moment with Him (because aren't we just always in such a hurry?). It's really important in our walk with Him to stop what we're doing and take that time. Don't just spend your "scheduled" time with Him. He wants more time with us. He wants us to talk and listen with Him. We can always find a reason for not doing this, but let's stop making excuses and let's start making more time. Be in that quiet moment with Him, and allow Him to refresh your mind and soul.

> Only fear the LORD and serve him faithfully with all your heart. For consider what great things he has done for you. 1 Samuel 12:24
> Complete my joy by being of the same mind, having the same love, being in full accord and of one mind. Philippians 2:2

Notes and Reflections

_____

_____

_____

Prayer
Dear Heavenly Father, thank You for the times I get to spend time with just You and me. Thank You for allowing me to know that I need to spend time with You and to just listen. I pray that I'm able to discern between my own thoughts and You speaking to me. In Jesus's name. Amen.

Growing

Learning to grow in Him has always been something I long for and work toward. I know many times I fail in my growth because of wanting to do it my way or just simply not listening. I've been reminded (especially lately) that my growth chart has hit a stumbling block and I need to get back into the nutrients that help me to grow—prayer, Bible reading, meditation, etc. It's these key ingredients that make up our daily walk with Him, and without these, our growth is stunted. Fellowship with others is also an important step in our growth. I try, but I'm a pretty strong introvert and don't really like big crowds. So with that being said, I have many ingredients I need to add to my life to be able to grow. How about you? What ingredients do you need to add?

> But grow in the grace and knowledge of our Lord and Savior Jesus Christ To Him be the glory, both now and to the day of eternity. 2 Peter 3:18
>
> So that Christ may dwell in your hearts through faith; and that you, being rooted and grounded in love, may be able to comprehend with all the saints what is the breadth and length and height and depth, and to know the love of Christ which surpasses knowledge, that you may be filled up to all the fullness of God. Ephesians 3:17–19

Notes and Reflections

_____

_____

_____

Prayer
Dear Heavenly Father, I know that my growing in You has taken detours more times than I care to admit, but I thank You for steering me back to where I need to be in my journey. Lord, You have given me the ingredients I need to grow in You and I thank You for never giving up on me. In Jesus's name. Amen.

The Littles

I've spent the last week taking care of two little ones. I noticed that their little minds never shut off and are always thinking of ways to do things or thinking of ways to get out of doing things. They bargained when I told them no and were happy when I said yes. And even in the midst of the chaotic days/nights, we had quiet time with reading, snuggles, hugs, and kisses. It's been a wonderful week. Our experience with our walk with God really isn't any different. When things aren't going our way, we bargain for that yes and pout because it hasn't come; and when we get what we want, we're so happy and say thank you (most times.) When I told my littles "no," it wasn't because I didn't want them to have something or not be able to do something; it's because I didn't want them to get hurt and it really wouldn't help them if I said yes. God is that way with us. He doesn't tell us no, or we feel that a prayer has gone unanswered because He wants to hurt us or upset us. It's because He knows what we need, when we need it, and if it's going to harm us; then a no will come in some fashion. Like my littles, they know I love them and only want them to be safe and happy. That's what God wants for us and to believe in Him. Spend the quiet time with Him, and see how your prayers are answered.

> Call to me and I will answer you, and will tell you great and hidden things that you have not known. Jeremiah 33:3

Notes and Reflections

_____

_____

_____

Prayer
Dear Heavenly Father, thank You for always knowing what I need and when I need it. You never let me fall and always have my best interest in Your hands. Thank You for continuously watching over me. In Jesus's name. Amen.

God's Music

This morning, I was awakened by the sound of thunder and rain. I laid there for a little while listening to God's sounds. He created everything, and yes, He even created storms. I love these sounds because they are very soothing; I enjoy them, and they're comforting. Isn't this the way we should look at everything God has created and when we are spending time with Him? To hear or see the perfection in it? To feel the comfort in knowing He created everything and is here with us? I've always said that the rain washes away the grunge of the world. It smells so fresh and clean after a rain, and our souls are at peace after time with Him. Our Father in Heaven created everything we see. It's up to us to take care of it and see the beauty. I try to see the beauty in everything (sometimes that doesn't work when I see a spider). However, I do try. God wants us to see His work—the beauty and the wonders. If you think about it, there are some pretty fascinating things out there, and He created them! The next time you look at something, really look at it and know that your God's hand is in the midst of it.

> In the beginning, God created the heavens and the earth. Genesis 1:1
>
> For by him all things were created, in heaven and on earth, visible and invisible, whether thrones or dominions or rulers or authorities—all things were created through him and for him. Colossians 1:16

Notes and Reflections

_____

_____

_____

Prayer

Dear Heavenly Father, thank You for the beautiful sounds I hear daily. I thank You for the freshness of the earth after a rain and for the beauty of everything created. Lord, please show me how to give You my time in realizing the intricate work You've done in us. In Jesus's name. Amen.

Mistakes

This morning, I was thinking about making mistakes and if God made a mistake when He created me. The answer to the second part of that statement is *no*. God didn't make a mistake when He created me or you. We were all created for a plan—His plan and His glory. Let's be honest, we've all had those moments in our lives when we thought, "God, why would you leave me here?" or "God, I really should have died, and we both know it." It's in those times we need to be thanking Him. We need to make that decision to live for Him. I say these things because I've had those moments (several, if I'm being honest). But knowing what I know now, God was with me all of the times I took chances I shouldn't have, and He was preparing me for who I am today. Some people I know would find a change in me hard to believe. But I was told yesterday, "I'm not who I say I am, but I *am* who He says I am." I love that! Remember who you are in Christ Jesus (you are not a mistake). Remember that you have a purpose here (you are not a mistake). He will show you where He wants you to be, and He will prepare you for it (He has a plan. You are not a mistake).

> But to all who have received him—those who believe in his name—he has given the right to become God's children. John 1:12

Notes and Reflections

_____

_____

_____

Prayer
Dear Heavenly Father, I know that I was created for a purpose and that I'm not a mistake. Show me how I can serve you in a way that will glorify You, and let others know that they are here for a purpose as well. We are all beautifully made in Your image. In Jesus's name. Amen.

Days for Him

Did you know that the calendar has "national days" for so many things? For example, there is Umbrella Day, Don't Cry Over Spilled Milk Day, National Gumdrop Day, Random Acts of Kindness Day, just to name a few. So what if every day were Christ Day and not just on Sunday? So every day we gave to the poor, helped the needy, spoke in Christlike fashion, worshipped and remained in prayer, etc. They would be days of peace and joy with no tears, no hunger, no abuse, etc. We shouldn't need a calendar to tell us that every day should be Christ Day. It's something we should do and the way we should be every day, all day long. Why should we need a calendar day to remind us of this? I know I'm guilty of not having Christ Days every day. There are days when, try as I might, I just don't let Him shine. I realize this and try to correct it. So let's try this today and every day; make them about Christ, living your life for Him in some fashion. Not only will it make *your* day better but someone else's as well.

> Do not neglect to do good and to share what you have, for such sacrifices are pleasing to God. Hebrews 13:16
> Let each of you look not only to his own interests, but also to the interests of others. Philippians 2:4

Notes and Reflections

_____

_____

_____

Prayer
Dear Heavenly Father, help me to remember that I shouldn't need to be reminded about spending time with You. I pray that I shouldn't spend time with You just on Sundays, but every day I should find quiet times to just simply be in Your presence. In Jesus's name. Amen.

Prayer

Prayer is an important part of our walk with our God. I'm guilty of not praying like I should because maybe something has happened in my life and I'm just not sure how to pray. I've also had someone tell me that they try to talk to God, but it doesn't always go well. Well, there's good news about this. It's all good. God knows our prayers before we ever speak them. I remember being told that if you think a prayer, it takes away from the actual prayer. But guess what? He already heard that prayer. Prayers don't have to be eloquent and go on forever. They just have to be from the heart, and they can be short. They can also be while you're driving in the car, flying on a plane, taking a walk, etc. Sometimes, at night, when I can't sleep, I sit up in bed and say, "Hey, God, it's me. I need to talk." And guess who shows up. That's right. God does. He listens to everything, and when I'm quiet, I can hear Him speaking to me. He just wants us to talk to Him and spend time with Him. Do this every day, throughout the day. You won't be sorry. It'll make your day even better than you can imagine. You'll have a peace like you've never imagined. Trust Him. Talk to Him.

> Praying at all times in the Spirit, with all prayer and supplication. To that end keep alert with all perseverance, making supplication for all the saints. Ephesians 6:18
>
> Pray without ceasing. 1 Thessalonians 5:17

Notes and Reflections
_____

_____

_____

Prayer
Dear precious Heavenly Father, I pray that I'm able to speak the words on my heart and that if I am unable, You will already know. Thank You for hearing my prayers even if I don't have the words in that moment. In Jesus's name. Amen.

Reflections

This morning has been a morning of reflection. Do you ever have those days when you really take time to reflect on your past, your present, and your future? This has been my morning. I've been thinking about where I've been, where I'm at, and where I'm going. My past (before Christ and even after) has all been a learning experience and will continue to be. While I didn't have a strong foundation when I first accepted Christ, it is being built, little by little, and today it's stronger than it used to be and will continue to gain strength.

Even though I've given so much of myself when I shouldn't have and I've made so many mistakes, I'm in awe that God would use me at all for the future. But while my past is more dull than colorful, it wasn't drawn and filled in with a permanent marker. He has taken those colors, erased them, and has colored my life with brighter colors, more brilliantly colorful than ever; and He continues to do so because you see, my past is gone, my present is building a stronger foundation in Him, and my future is brighter with Him. Yours is too. Just think about it, and allow Him to build on your foundation and color your life. It's brilliantly amazing!

> Therefore, if anyone is in Christ, the new creation has come: [a] The old has gone, the new is here! 2 Corinthians 5:17
>
> Therefore everyone who hears these words of mine and puts them into practice is like a wise man who built his house on the rock. The rain came down, the streams rose, and the winds blew and beat against that house; yet it did not fall, because it had its foundation on the rock. But everyone who hears these words of mine and does not put them into practice is like a foolish man who built his house on sand. The rain came down, the streams rose, and the winds blew and beat against that house, and it fell with a great crash. Matthew 7:24–27

Notes and Reflections

_____

_____

_____

Prayer

Dear Heavenly Father, thank You for the quiet times You give me so that I may reflect on my life. I thank You that my life wasn't drawn with a permanent marker and that You are the one who erases our mistakes. I pray I may live my life in a way that is colorful and beautiful because of Your love. In Jesus's name. Amen.

Blessings

Have you ever found "something" that you didn't know you had at the right time it was needed? I call those times blessings. They come in many ways and at times when we least expect them. This morning at the store, I watched a young mother being blessed with the cashier taking money from her own purse to pay the $1.35 she needed to finalize her purchase. This touched my heart because, as a former cashier, I saw a lot of need in this. I know some will think that it's done for the "compliments" that come after. I can tell you this is not the case. For me, I've been there. I know how it feels to lack a few coins and have someone bless me like that. We all have something in our life or a have had a time in our life when a blessing (big or small) has come, and it just touches our hearts, and it doesn't matter if a blessing comes from someone we know or a stranger. God shows up in many ways, and when we bless someone, do it with a happy heart (not because you want through the checkout). Do it with the right mindset. Be that blessing someone needed today. It makes God smile.

> And my God will supply all your needs according to His riches in glory in Christ Jesus. Philippians 4:19
>
> Whatever you do, do your work heartily, as for the Lord rather than for men. Colossians 3:23

Notes and Reflections

_____

_____

_____

Prayer
Dear Heavenly Father, thank You for the many blessings I've seen and those I received when I didn't realize I needed one. I pray that in some way, I may be a blessing to someone and that I remain mindful of why we do things for others. In Jesus's name. Amen.

Trust

Sometimes—actually, more often than not—when things happen in our lives, our minds go to the worst possible place. When my mom was having her last surgery for a tumor that had strategically attached itself to the aorta in her back, I immediately went into "medical mode" and started researching. Instead of just giving it to God and knowing He would take care of everything (which He did), my mind went to the dark side of things. I think this is natural at times because of our schooling or similar things that happened in our lives. But the truth of the matter is this: God already had this under control. He had gone before my mom, was waiting on her at the hospital, and had already prepared the surgeons and nurses for this surgery. He does that in our lives if we can just get to that place of faith and let Him in.

Today, if you are having an issue in your life, just stop and take a moment and give it to God. He's there, waiting. He already knows, but again, He's waiting on our faith in Him to bring us to that moment with Him. Go there. I finally did, and I continue to thank Him for the healing in my mom then and for the healing He continues to do in her and me.

> Those who hope in the LORD will renew their strength. They will soar on wings like eagles; they will run and not grow weary, they will walk and not be faint. Isaiah 40:31

Notes and Reflections

_____

_____

_____

Prayer
Dear Heavenly Father, I ask that You take my thoughts into captivity and allow me to remain positive when things begin to look dark. I pray that I'm mindful of putting all of my trust in You and knowing You are the Almighty Healer in every way and part of my life. I pray that my faith in You remain each and every day. In Jesus's name. Amen.

Faith

Yesterday's sermon talked about getting out of the boat, having faith, and following Jesus. Could you do that? I've always thought about that question. If Jesus was on the street today and He said, "Come," would I? Would you? Would you be able to leave your family, friends, things you hold dear to your heart, etc.? I have always said, "I would like to think that I would drop everything and follow Him. No doubt." But the truth is, Could I? Would I? We value things today that, in our minds, would be huge sacrifices to give up. But think about this: He sacrificed His life for us. He gave Himself, so why wouldn't we give up the material things of this world and follow Him? I know one day we will spend eternity with Him, but how amazing would it be to spend every day with Him now? But really, we can spend every day with Him in other ways other than the physical—reading the Word of God, praying, church, and living our lives for Him. So really, we can come and follow Him now by doing those things—things that bring Him honor and glory and things that keep our relationship with Him so strong that nothing can come between us. Be a follower of Christ. There's nothing standing in your way.

> May the Lord direct your hearts into God's love and Christ's perseverance. 2 Thessalonians 3:5

Notes and Reflections

_____

_____

_____

Prayer
Dear Heavenly Father, I pray that I'm able to get out of the boat and say "yes and amen" to the things You would have me to do in Your name. I pray that each time You ask me to follow You, I say "yes" without any doubts or fears. I lift each day up to You that I may easily go with You. In Jesus's name. Amen.

Our Future

This morning, I listened to a commercial that was advertising a psychic, and the women were so happy that the psychic told them that they would find their "true love" or that they would find the "perfect job." Well, confession time. I went to one psychic in particular for several years (spent a lot of money). I won't pretend that I didn't believe everything she said to me, but then when her "predictions" didn't come true, I was heartbroken. I thought, "How can this be?" But the truth is, there is no one that can predict your future except one, and it's not a prediction. It's the truth. God is the only one that knows our future, what we will go through, and the outcome. He has known us from before we were even conceived. To me, that is pretty amazing and wonderful. The fact that He knows me so well is enough for me because this is where my faith comes in. If we could go to someone and have them predict our future, then where's the faith? We need to go to Him for our here and now and leave the future to Him. He knows. He knows what we need and when we need it, and He knows the outcome. And it doesn't cost us a thing because He has already paid the price for us—for our sins, our here and now, and our future.

> For I know the plans I have for you, declares the Lord, plans for welfare and not for evil, to give you a future and a hope. Jeremiah 29:11

Notes and Reflections

_____

_____

_____

Prayer
Dear Heavenly Father, I pray for Your guidance and direction in my life and that with each new day, I am able to see all that You have in store for me. I pray that never doubt my future and the plans You have for my life and that I'm trusting in You to show me the way. In Jesus's name. Amen.

Stand On It!

I remember in nursing school, an instructor always told us that when we answer a question and we just know it's right, we need to *stand on it*! I always liked that phrase because I knew that if I was that sure about something, why not own it? I think this is especially true when it comes to our faith in Christ. How many times have you not been as enthusiastic about your answer to questions concerning our Father in heaven as you want to be because, really, you feel like you know the answer but there's that little bit of hesitation as you second-guess yourself, and if you're the least little bit off, then, hmm, what would that person think about you and your faith walk? I'm here to tell you that none of us is perfect. However, when you just know it, you just know it. Don't second-guess yourself. God will bring forth what you need in these situations, and so just allow that to happen. So here's my suggestion to you, and I know I need to follow it as well: Stand up for what you believe in and know about the Lord and His Word. Don't allow others to try and sway you or even stump you in what you believe and your understanding of the Word. Know it, own it, show it, and stand on it!

> All scripture is God-breathed and is useful for teaching, rebuking, correcting and training in righteousness, so that the servant of God may be thoroughly equipped for every good work. 2 Timothy 3:16–17, NIV
>
> The unfolding of your words gives light; it gives understanding to the simple. Psalm 119:130, NIV

Notes and Reflections

_____

_____

_____

Prayer

Dear Heavenly Father, I pray that I may be bold in standing on Your Word and in Your Word. I pray that I am able to bring scripture to remembrance when needed and be able to share with others. In Jesus's name. Amen.

Our Journey

My life's journey has changed a lot over the past few years. Some would say "not really" or "not enough" or something else along those lines, and you know what? It's okay. I still have my bad days. The road is bumpy, but it doesn't make me a horrible person or a bad Christian. It makes me human. I make mistakes, I get down, and I even say things that I shouldn't. But I'm thankful that in Christ and His grace, I'm forgiven. We should always strive for a Christlike attitude and life, but the truth of the matter is that we *all* fall short of the glory of God. But our journey is His, and it's beautiful. There are so many ways to help us in our journey, but the greatest of them all is Him and His Word. I encourage you to get your Bible out, dust it off, open it up, and begin reading. There's no right or wrong place to begin because it's all amazingly wonderful! Before you read, ask God to open your mind and heart to His Word. He will show you things you never knew. My journey has been long in getting where I am today. It's not been easy, but it's been worth it. When I see where I've come from to where I'm at today, it makes me thankful for Him never giving up on me and for the people in my life who have helped me in my walk with Him and who continue to walk/run with me. Make your journey beautiful with Him.

> But he said to them, "Do not detain me, now that the LORD has granted success to my journey. Send me on my way so I may go to my master." Genesis 24:56

Notes and Reflections

_____

_____

_____

Prayer

Dear Heavenly Father, I thank You for the journey I've been on because I know that You have been with me all along the way. I pray that my attitude reflects the change in me. I thank You for never giving up on me and for showing me how amazing my life can be in following You. In Jesus's name. Amen.

Expectations

Expectations are something we all have, and they're about what we think our lives should be, possibly at the age we are now. But how many of those expectations were obtainable? All of them? Some of them? How many of those expectations lined up with Him? All of them? Some of them? None of them? Expectations can be daunting, and in fact, they can take over how we approach things. However, when we let go of what we perceive the outcome should be and just give our desires to Him, the outcome can and will be so much more than we expected. I used to always say that I didn't expect things to be great because then I wouldn't be disappointed when they weren't. I went about that all wrong. I'm learning that, day by day. Our walk with God should have the expectation of greatness. We should expect our prayers to be answered in some fashion (sometimes they aren't answered in the way we expected); we should expect that God will always give us what we need when we need it. Expect Him to meet us where we live, and expect Him to be God in our lives. He has certain expectations from us too, though, to follow Him, spend time in prayer with Him, read His Word, and live as close as we can to a Christlike life. So go ahead. Expect Him to work in your lives. He will. And just see how your expectations come alive!

> For God alone, O my soul, wait in silence, for my hope is from him. Psalm 62:5

Notes and Reflections
_____

_____

_____

Prayer
Dear Heavenly Father, I know that I should always expect You to do great things in my life. My life hasn't gone as I expected it to, but I know it's gone the way You had planned for me. Thank You for always knowing what's best for me. In Jesus's name. Amen.

Helping Others

I had an incident (three times) this week where I had to do something I didn't feel was my job to do. Well, this morning I had to brush off my car (thank you, Mother Nature), and I heard this voice in my head saying, "You need to brush off her car too." I battled with this voice for a while and then finally realized, "Why am I battling this? He knows I'm going to do it because that's who I am." Why wouldn't I want to help someone out? I mean, it's the right thing to do; I should have just done it and not had to be reminded. But as I'm brushing it off, knowing where my heart should be in doing so, my thought process wasn't where it should have been. I knew afterward that it probably helped her more than I will know. She has two littles that she cares for alone, and many times, I can hear her frustration. So why wouldn't I want to help make her load just a little lighter even if in just a small way? God puts people in our path to help, to encourage, and to bless. He knows we get discouraged at times, but it's up to us to rise above that discouragement and continue on as Christ's followers and do the work of our Father. My lesson in this is that I may not always enjoy doing the task at hand for others, but it's my attitude in doing the task that matters. I may not want to smile while working, but I know in my heart it's right, so that makes me smile even if but a small grin. Don't let your frustrations get in the way of becoming a blessing to someone. You never know what they're battling.

Notes and Reflections

_____

_____

_____

Prayer
Dear Heavenly Father, thank You for giving me the capabilities to help others in need even when I don't feel like You give me the know-how and strength. Thank You for helping me to check my attitude and know that I should be helping others in a way that brings You praise and glory. In Jesus's name. Amen.

Creation

I'm watching the National Geographic Channel, and each time I do, I'm fascinated even more by the world that God created. So many believe that this world was created by a loud *bang*! Well, guess what? That's not the case. How could a *bang* create the hundreds of species of butterflies and birds and frogs and so many other animals? I was amazed at the salmon shark (didn't know there was one). It swims in the freezing ocean by Alaska. They explained that the way the water filters through the fins and the blood is oxygenated, and it warms the body temp up to 68 degrees above the freezing water. Now, I ask you, How can that intricate creation be anything other than God? I think, for me, I always knew that God created the heavens and earth and everything else, but my mind didn't go to *all* that He created—so colorful, so different, and so important to the cycle of life. I've heard a saying, "God is like the wind. You can't see Him, but you can feel Him." Well, no, because you see, we *can* see and feel Him. He is seen in everything created, which just happens to be absolutely everything you see and even the spaces in space we can't see. His hand is in everything. He is felt when you feel His peace, love, and joy flow through you during prayer or when you feel Him as others pray for you. Don't ever think that this life was created by anything or anyone other than Him. You are Him, and He is in you. You are a beautiful, intricate, colorful creation.

> The Spirit of God hath made me, and the breath of the Almighty hath given me life. Job 33:4
> For by him all things were created, in heaven and on earth, visible and invisible, whether thrones or dominions or rulers or authorities—all things were created through him and for him. Colossians 1:16

Notes and Reflections

_____

_____

_____

Prayer

Dear Heavenly Father, thank You for everything so brilliantly created by You. Thank You for the intricate work that is in all of us and in everything You created. Teach me, Lord, that I should take the time to stop and look at Your handiwork and the colors You so brilliantly display in everything. In Jesus's name. Amen.

Everything

When was the last time you really not only looked to Father for everything going on in your life but looked to Him to *be* the everything in your life? To guide you, to open the right door, to close the wrong door, and to allow people in your life that will nurture you and remove those who don't? When I think about these things, I can see so many changes taking place, not only in my life but in the lives of others. For me, one major change has been that I've started meditating again (much needed), and another new change is that I have my Bible now open at my desk; and when I start feeling the weight of the world, I look over and read a few scriptures. It's very calming. It's the little things that He gives us, and we don't even realize maybe that it's Him that helps guide us along the way. I randomly opened my Bible to Acts and began reading. I've already begun to read things that I've missed from the last time I read it, *or* it could be that He is opening my mind and eyes to see something different. Either way, He's in this. Pray about ways you can change up your time with Him. Look to Him to be your guide through this life because after all, it's really His life, but He's given us the ultimate of instruction books.

> But from there you will seek the Lord your God and you will find him, if you search after him with all your heart and with all your soul. Deuteronomy 4:29

Notes and Reflections

_____

_____

_____

Prayer
Dear Heavenly Father, I thank You for being not only my everything but being in everything in my life. I pray that I may make the time to spend with You and in Your presence. I'm thankful that I am at a place where it's okay to read Your Word throughout the day and not be persecuted for it. In Jesus's name. Amen.

Heartbeats

Being an RN and not able to practice medically hasn't been an easy adjustment for me to accept. It's been heartbreaking to say the least, and yet while I know God put me in the medical field, it helps to know He still has a plan for me to use this in some way. With that being said, a good friend said to me one day, as I was voicing my bitterness about this, "I'm still listening to heartbeats, just a different kind." I asked her what she meant, and she said, "You're still listening to people's hearts, but just without a stethoscope." This spoke volumes to me. She was right. Even though I'm not working in the hospital or clinic, every day I'm listening to someone's heart (the way they feel, their hopes, dreams, etc.). I'm sharing my heart with others as well. So if I'm looking at the "big picture," I'm still listening, just in a better way. God has put something on my heart, and it allows me to be a better listener; and while it's not in a medical way, I'm still listening. When you listen to the heartbeats of others, really open your mind to what they are saying, heartbeats speak volumes.

> Know this, my beloved brothers: let every person be quick to hear, slow to speak, slow to anger. James 1:19
>
> Making your ear attentive to wisdom and inclining your heart to understanding. Proverbs 2:2

Notes and Reflections

_____

_____

_____

Prayer
Dear Heavenly Father, I thank You that I am able to hear the heartbeats not only of myself but of others in my life. I pray that when I hear the cries and joys of others, I am able to cry or rejoice with them and know that it doesn't matter what instrument I'm using to hear them, a strong heartbeat in You. In Jesus's name. Amen.

Behavior

Isn't it funny how we have "learned behavior" but some of our behavior is just natural? Negativity, for example, is such an easy behavior as to where finding the positive can be a challenge at times. I find this as I go through my daily life. Yes, I'm more positive than I was a couple of years ago, but if I'm not careful, my negativity will show quicker than you can blink, and it takes me back. I don't want to be there. I want the positive Christ in me. When Christ is in us, shouldn't we want to remain positive at all times? I know it's difficult, and He knows we aren't perfect, but that's why we have grace and forgiveness. He covers us. He forgives us. Make your new "learned behavior" positive. It will soon become "who you are" and not a struggle to be.

> What you have learned and received and heard and seen in me—practice these things, and the God of peace will be with you. Philippians 4:9
>
> And he who sent me is with me. He has not left me alone, for I always do the things that are pleasing to him. John 8:29

Notes and Reflections

_____

_____

_____

Prayer
Dear Heavenly Father, I pray that my behavior reflects that of the Christ that is in me and not the negativity of the world. I pray that with each day, I'm able to remain positive in the midst of life, knowing that You are right there with me. I pray, Lord, that my struggle be light in a new behavior. In Jesus's name. Amen.

Words

Today was a day that I had a chance to be a non-Christian to use my past words and attitude to yell at someone. Instead, I chose to rise above the situation, and I chose my words carefully. I could hear in my mind the scripture James 1:19: "My dear brothers and sisters, take note of this: Everyone should be quick to listen, slow to speak and slow to become angry." Now, I had to take several deep breaths and calm myself before speaking, but this scripture helped me tremendously. Father knows we will have trials here on earth. In fact, it says so in His Word. But I know He is with me, and He helped guide my words today. If you're struggling with words, just stop, close your eyes, and talk to Him. He's right there, and if you listen, you can hear the words He wants you to speak.

> Blessed is the man who remains steadfast under trial, for when he has stood the test he will receive the crown of life, which God has promised to those who love him. James 1:12

Notes and Reflections

_____

_____

_____

Prayer
Dear Heavenly Father, thank You for keeping Your hand on my shoulder and allowing You to shine through. Thank You for allowing me to hear You and for guiding my steps and words. In Jesus's name. Amen.

A Change of Heart/Mind

Sometimes our heart hurts because something is going on or has happened, it upsets us, and we don't feel like we'll ever get past it. This is because we begin with our mind, in our thinking, and our feelings; and when our mind "fixes" it, then we think our heart heals. Father works on us differently. He begins with our hearts, and then He works on our minds because, you see, when you have a change of heart, you have a change of mind and thought process. When we pray for a change, it has to be a change of heart first. When we pray for a renewed spirit, it has to be a renewed heart first. Everything begins with the heart. If it's ugly, then so are our thoughts. When you talk to Him, ask Him for a change of heart. Ask Him to allow your heart to hear, feel, and hurt because by doing that, you're asking Him for many other changes in your life. I've asked so many times for a change of heart, especially when I get hurt. Being hurt can be one of the most difficult heart/mind changes that need to happen. I wanted to stay mad because it allowed me to keep my guard up, and with my guard up, I could control the hurt and who I allowed in. But He has a better way. When I allowed Him to change my heart, then not only did my thinking change, but my life changed. I'm going through some changes in my life as I write this, and I know that He will be there ready to change my heart/mind, and it will all be good and for His glory. Ask Him for a change. He will make many; you will see a new you, and it's amazing!

> Therefore if anyone is in Christ, he is a new creature; the old things passed away; behold, new things have come. 2 Corinthians 5:17
>
> I will give them a heart to know Me, for I am the LORD; and they will be My people, and I will be their God, for they will return to Me with their whole heart. Jeremiah 24:7
>
> Create in me a clean heart, O God, And renew a steadfast spirit within me. Psalm 51:10

Notes and Reflections

_____

_____

_____

Prayer

Dear Heavenly Father, I lift my heart and mind up to You, and I thank You for the changes You have made in me. I know that You are in control, and I thank You for never giving up on me. In Jesus's name. Amen.

Sin

It seems that in today's world, sin is taken too lightly. We seem to do the same thing over and over again, and while we're in sin, we don't, at that moment, think about the price that was paid for us. Tonight, I watched *The Passion of the Christ*. I have to tell you that this is the most powerful movie you can ever see. Think about every drop of blood that He shed while being beaten, while He was carrying the cross, and even while they were getting ready to nail Him to the cross. The crown of thorns that wasn't just placed on His head; it was put there with enough force that the thorns went into his head. I cried as I watched this because I knew that for all the pain He endured, it was because of my sins. I found myself, during the movie, asking for forgiveness. We sin, not realizing the brutality that our Savior went through so that we may be saved and have eternal life. I can't even fathom how much worse it was for Him during that time. The next time we think about sinning, stop, think about the one who died for that sin, and then think again.

> If anyone, then, knows the good they ought to do and doesn't do it, it is sin for them. James 4:17

Notes and Reflections

_____

_____

_____

Prayer
Dear Heavenly Father, thank You for the sacrifice You made for my sins. There are no words that can describe how sorry I am for all of my sins. I thank You for Your forgiveness and for Your grace and mercy. I pray, Lord, that in my sinful nature, I remember how much You gave so that I could be forgiven. I thank You in Jesus's name. Amen.

Lessons

Have you ever wondered why life lessons have to be so painful? I know I do. I remember being told, in my younger years, I was the stubborn child. It didn't matter how many times I was corrected; I would do the same thing over and over again. (I'm still pretty hardheaded.) But in a loving manner, I finally got it. Do you ever wonder if Father is thinking, "How many times are they going to before they get it?" I always wonder about that, and I sometimes think He is up there, shaking His head at me and saying, "Oh, will she ever get it?" But then there are times when I know He has to be disappointed in me because I haven't "gotten it." The lessons He teaches us aren't meant to cause us harm or to hurt us but to strengthen us and draw us closer to Him. I realize at times, it takes us longer than it should, but when it happens and we finally do get it, *wow*! The end result from the lesson learned is amazing. I always say, "I always hear what I'm being taught. I just haven't learned it yet." I know the sooner I learn, the better I'll be in my relationship with Him. Don't take too long to learn the lessons. He is waiting.

> Whoever heeds discipline shows the way to life, but whoever ignores correction leads others astray. Proverbs 10:17

Notes and Reflections
___
___
___

Prayer
Dear Heavenly Father, thank You for the life lessons and the patience You've had with me in learning them. I know that I can be trying and Your love and patience with me never wavers. Lord, I am being taught each and every day, and I am thankful for each and every lesson learned. I pray that I understand what You are teaching and am able to continue to learn. In Jesus's name. Amen.

Eternity

Have you ever thought about living your life for the eternity that is to come? The statement was made this week: "I don't live my life for eternity." My question is this: Why not? Shouldn't we live each day as if it's the day that Christ will return and we will begin our eternal life with Him? That when we go before Him, He will say, "Well done, my good and faithful servant"? I'm not sure if every day I think about that statement or if I live like it. To me, it's saying that I'm not living my life now as I should live every day for Him, I'm not doing what He would have me do, and I'm not being who He would have me be. I sometimes forget Whom I'm living for and that what I'm doing should bring Him glory and honor. So think about it. Think about that life with Him—eternal life.

> For God so loved the world that he gave his one and only Son, that whoever believes in him shall not perish but have eternal life. John 3:16
>
> Give them eternal life, and they shall never perish; no one will snatch them out of my hand. My Father, who has given them to me, is greater than all; no one can snatch them out of my Father's hand. I and the Father are one. John 10:28–30

Notes and Reflections

_____

_____

_____

Prayer
Dear Heavenly Father, I pray that I can continue to live my life for You and for my final destination. I pray that I am living and knowing that in the end, You will be there waiting. Thank You for giving us eternal life with You. In Jesus's name. Amen.

Surrender

This morning, during my prayer time, I was reminded that it was time for me to surrender everything to Him. I find this difficult to do as there is "life" that I'm not ready to let go of and isn't that the way it is? We want it all, but we don't want to give up everything. We want to give Him our struggles and sins, but then we take them back. So surrendering everything to Him would be giving Him my everything—sins, anxieties, worries, fears, my life. My life for Him to change. My life for Him to have 100 percent control over. We find many reasons not to allow this to happen. We can fix it ourselves, I just need time, etc. But the truth is this: He can fix it much better than we can, His timing is perfect, and the outcome will be greater than anything we can even begin to comprehend. By surrendering everything to Him, you're saying, "Okay, God, let's go. I'm ready." I would like to say that I'm one-hundred-percent ready, but I'm being honest here. I'm not. Will I surrender everything to Him? Absolutely, and it will be sooner rather than later. I'm ready and excited for everything He is doing and will do in my life. I just need to take that step. So ask yourselves this: Will I take that step today? Will I surrender? He's waiting.

> Surrender your heart to God, turn to him in prayer, and give up your sins—even those you do in secret. Then you won't be ashamed; you will be confident and fearless. Job 11:13–15

Notes and Reflections

_____

_____

_____

Prayer
Dear Heavenly Father, I pray that I am able to surrender all to You and not hold back. I pray that I don't take back the things I have given You to take from me. I pray that sooner rather than later, I can, without reservation, give You my all. In Jesus's name. Amen.

Toolbox

Toolboxes come in every size, shape, and color. They all contain different tools that are needed to fix what's broken. There is another toolbox I wonder about people having in their homes—the spiritual toolbox. This toolbox is more important than any other, and it contains everything, not only what you need to fix what's broken in your life and within yourself but to grow in your relationship with Him. Do you have one? I do, but I don't always open it up because sometimes, I'm sorry to say, I have to remove the dust. However, my toolbox contains the following: a Bible, to read about how much Father loves me and wants a relationship with me; a journal, to write my thoughts and prayers down; meditation time, to just spend time quietly with Him and meditate on His Word; a phone number, for someone I can have Christian fellowship with and know that they aren't judging me but instead loving me no matter how big of a mess I am; and lastly, but just as important, a prayer, to talk with Him and allow Him to fix my brokenness. Each toolbox could contain other things as well, but for me, these are important for my walk with Him. Do I utilize each one daily? Unfortunately no, as I said before, but each day I strive to do better than the day before. Open the toolbox He has given you, and allow what's broken to be repaired and your walk to be closer to Him than ever before.

> Therefore I tell you, whatever you ask in prayer, believe that you have received it, and it will be yours. Mark 11:24

Notes and Reflections
_____
_____
_____

Prayer
Dear Heavenly Father, thank You for the many tools you give me to get through my day. I thank You for the most important tool of all, Your Word. I pray that I remember everything I need is in that one book. In Jesus's name. Amen.

Our Destination

I listened to Tony Evans talk about reaching our destination, lining up with Him to get there, and being able to hear God. He spoke about how it's like we have an antenna on top of our heads. If they're bent, then we can't get good reception, and then in which case, we can't hear Him. When we can't hear Him, then it's difficult to get our lives to line up with His will. I've always been excited when I hear Him speak to me. Sometimes it's a lengthy conversation, but sometimes it's just a few words. When I allow the noise and stuff of this world to "bend my antenna" and I can't hear Him, I get frustrated. Lately I've had a personal issue going on, and so it's been cloudy, and my antenna hasn't been able to pick up on anything He may have wanted to say to me. But this week, I've heard Him loud and clear. I didn't even realize my antenna had been readjusted, but He helps us do that. The thing is, when we shut out the noise, He becomes so much more clearer. And when that happens, it's so amazingly wonderful. In the time I needed to hear Him, He spoke to me (His timing). God is good! Don't allow this world to dictate what/who you hear, but rather, allow Him to enter into your space and straighten those antennas. He wants to speak to you, and He wants you to hear Him.

> For the word of God is living and active, sharper than any two-edged sword, piercing to the division of soul and of spirit, of joints and of marrow, and discerning the thoughts and intentions of the heart. Hebrews 4:12, ESV

Notes and Reflections

_____

_____

_____

Prayer

Dear Heavenly Father, I pray that the noise of life be filtered out, that I am able to remain focused on You, and that I am able to hear what You would say to me. I pray that when I need to hear You, You make the way for that to happen. In Jesus's name. Amen.

My Story

We all have a story. Some stories are harder to hear than others, but all are just as important because they've made us into who we are today. But with every story, Father already knows how it will go, how it will end, and whether or not you turn it around now or later. If your story isn't where you want it to be, if it doesn't have the meat of who you are, and if it isn't working the way you thought it would, then rewrite it. Rewrite your story so that it includes our Father in heaven. Rewrite it so it includes the best book ever written as your guide. Rewrite it so it includes a life in eternity with Him. Rewrite it and begin now, not tomorrow. Some of the best books written took quite a long time. Your story, like theirs, can take years to write but overnight to change it and begin a new chapter. Life will be full of new stories with new chapters and new journeys to write about and live. But don't forget to include our Savior in your story. After all, He's the reason we are here, and our story should be a tell-all about our life of coming to know Him, where He takes us and where He will take us. It can truly be an adventure if we just open ourselves up to Him. I encourage you to not keep your story to yourself. Share it and tell others your story, and tell them about the Christ in you that has been with you throughout your journey. I think my story/book would be titled *Daily Thoughts* because with each one I write, they're a reflection of my life, where He has taken me and where He will take me. They may not always be as good as the one before, but I guarantee you, each one tells my story, a new chapter, and a new journey.

> Tell it to your children, and let your children tell it to their children, and their children to the next generation. Joel 1:3

Notes and Reflections

_____

_____

_____

Prayer

Dear Heavenly Father, I pray that the story of my life contains You in the heart of it all. I thank You for my story and how it's unfolding before me. Thank You for each story and chapter of my life. In Jesus's name. Amen.

The Race: Part 1

I watched a movie clip played about Secretariat. In case you don't follow horse racing, Secretariat was a triple crown winner. While I was watching, I could feel the excitement building as I watched one of the most magnificent of God's creatures, running, focused, and never looking behind; and at times with all four hooves off of the ground, I could feel it in my belly. I was thinking, "C'mon, Secretariat, you can do it. C'mon!" And of course, even though I knew the outcome already, I was still on the edge of my seat with tears in my eyes as I watched him win. I sometimes miss that excitement building—focused, running, never looking back, feet off the ground, fire in my belly for the Lord. We sit on the sidelines (in the stands) and cheer everyone on instead of, like Secretariat, run a race that will have the most beautiful ending ever when we finish it in heaven. If we focus, not allow ourselves to look back, and allow our feet off the ground, that excitement will come. It'll be that "fire in your belly" that you miss. I miss it. We tend to want to take the easy way to get things done instead of building and savoring that feeling of excitement as we learn more about Him, begin saying yes and amen, and know we're about to enter and win the most important race of our lives. Don't sit in the stands and watch others. Run the race. Run toward Him. Don't look back and never give up.

> Do you not know that in a race all the runners run, but only one receives the prize? So run that you may obtain it. 1 Corinthians 9:24, ESV
>
> Therefore we also, since we are surrounded by so great a cloud of witnesses, let us lay aside every weight, and the sin which so easily ensnares us, and let us run with endurance the race that is set before us, looking unto Jesus, the author and finisher of our faith, who for the joy that was set before Him endured the cross, despising the shame, and has sat down at the right hand of the throne of God. Hebrews 12:1–2, NKJV

Notes and Reflections

_____

_____

_____

Prayer

Dear Heavenly Father, thank You for the daily encouragement in knowing my race is just beginning and for allowing me to know the outcome at the end. I pray that I continue to run toward You as the excitement builds in knowing You are at the end of this race I am currently running. In Jesus's name. Amen.

The Race: Part 2

So as Secretariat ran his hardest and kept his focus on the finish line, shouldn't we be doing that same thing in our walk with Him? Secretariat, however, didn't do it alone. He had a trainer and a jockey to help steer him in the right direction and make sure he stayed on track. We have that in Christ. We have His book (the Bible) to teach us, and it allows us to train in that we can do all things through Him that gives us our strength. Through prayer, He helps steer us in the right direction and guides our every step. In that, we should want to stay on track and win this amazing race called life and know that the finish line is within focus and reach. I know that, for me, I've taken the long way around in getting out of the gate and running the race with Him. But with each turn of the corner and day that goes by, I know my race is in step with Him. I know that He is guiding me and not allowing me to look back but to keep looking ahead at the finish line.

> Let us run with endurance the race God has set before us. Hebrews 12:1
>
> Commit everything you do to the Lord. Trust him, and he will help you. Psalm 37:5

Notes and Reflections
_____
_____
_____

Prayer:
Dear Heavenly Father, some days I struggle to stay on track, but I thank You for being there, cheering me on as I continue this amazing race of life. Thank You for not giving up on me and for guiding and directing each and every step. In Jesus's name. Amen.

The Race: Part 3, the Final Stretch

When Secretariat passed, they performed an autopsy. One thing that stood out was that his heart was bigger than a normal heart, and one thing is for sure: he ran his race with the fullness of that heart, and he gave them his all. He gave full control and trust to the jockey to lead him where he needed to go and finished strong. Shouldn't we do that? Let God have full control because He wants to lead us to victory in Him. He wants to show us His ways, but we need to get out of the way and give Him the reins. Secretariat had a big heart not only physically but mentally when it came to racing, and he loved it. We should have a bigger heart for God. We should be physically and mentally ready to take on any race and allow Him to pump our hearts full of His love and encouragement. In the final stretch, he gave all he had. In *our* final stretch, we need to give all that we have—run that race for our God. At the end, allow Him to say, "Well done, my good and faithful servant." See, it's not enough to just run the race. We need to train; we need to give Him the lead, follow Him, never look back, keep our hearts and minds focused, keep our eyes on the finish line, and run strong with a heart that's bigger than big. He has equipped us, and we are ready. Let God take the reins. Trust Him in running your race. Feel the "sitting on the edge of your seat excitement" of running toward Him. Finish hard, and finish *strong*!

> Do you not know that in a race all the runners run, but only one gets the prize? Run in such a way as to get the prize. 1 Corinthians 9:24, NIV
>
> Therefore, since we are surrounded by so great a cloud of witnesses, let us also lay aside every weight, and sin which clings so closely, and let us run with endurance the race that is set before us. Hebrews 12:1, ESV

Notes and Reflections

_____

_____

_____

Prayer

Dear Heavenly Father, I pray that my heart remain bigger than normal in my love not only for You but for others. I pray that in my final stretch of life, I know that I was able to give my all in running this amazing race called life. In Jesus's name. Amen.

Quiet Time

When I first began these, I quieted myself and waited. I waited for my mind to block out the noise of the day, and I waited for Father to speak to me because you see, these words aren't mine. They're His. I didn't realize it's been ten days since my last post. That's the thing about life. It comes and goes, and you don't realize time has gone by and some things don't get done. They maybe don't feel like a priority. It's not that I don't make Father a priority, but I don't always allow Him to have that place in my daily life. When this happens, I get a "feeling" about it. It's like He is saying, "Um, we haven't spent time together. We need to spend time together." So I listen, and I'm always glad I did. But the thing is, we shouldn't have to be reminded by Him to spend time with Him. It should absolutely be a priority in our day. When you don't make Him a priority, your day really isn't what it should be, nor is it what it could be. He can take your day and turn it into something so amazing. Isn't that what you would want to happen? Having a great amazing day with Him? Well, He wants to have that amazing day with you. So allow yourself that time with Him—early morning, lunchtime, evening, before bedtime—but the truth of the matter is that you can spend any time of the day with Him. He's always there.

> Devote yourselves to prayer, being watchful and thankful.
> Colossians 4:2

Notes and Reflections

_____

_____

_____

Prayer
Dear Heavenly Father, thank You for giving my thoughts that I may share them with others who may be going through the same life issues as I am. I pray that just one can relate, and I pray that they are relieved to know that someone else is going through the same thing and has found peace in You. In Jesus's name. Amen.

Anxiety

It seems, lately, that Satan has been hard at work in my life, and this morning was no different. As I got up and tried starting my day, it got worse, and soon I was thrown into a full-blown anxiety attack. Have you ever had that happen? I immediately texted my sisters and asked them to pray. I sat on my couch and began praying. Before I knew it, I felt a peace like no other. The sun was so warm on my face; I knew it could only be Him. Through tears during prayer, I knew I would be okay because He has me and won't let me fall.

Did my anxiety return? Yes, to a point. Not because He didn't still have me but because I took my eyes off of Him for a few moments. You see, when we keep our focus on Him, there is nothing that He can't get us through, and Satan can't get to us. Don't let the fears and anxieties of life win. I don't. But I'll be honest. I do have to medicate daily, and that's okay. Father has given us doctors and medicine to help in every illness, and yes, it's okay that we use them. But we must also remember that He is our true healer. We can be healed in so many ways, inside and out.

Remember to take your worries, fears, and well, life to Him. He's got you. He'll not let you fall, and He never gives up on us. He's there always.

> Do not be anxious about anything, but in everything by prayer and supplication with thanksgiving let your requests be made known to God. And the peace of God, which surpasses all understanding, will guard your hearts and your minds in Christ Jesus. Philippians 4:6–7
>
> Humble yourselves, therefore, under the mighty hand of God so that at the proper time he may exalt you, casting all your anxieties on him, because he cares for you. 1 Peter 5:6–7
>
> The God of peace will soon crush Satan under your feet. The grace of our Lord Jesus Christ be with you. Romans 16:20

Notes and Reflections

_____

_____

_____

Prayer

Dear Heavenly Father, thank You for watching over me during the times of my anxiety issues and for the peace I can feel through You. I know it's always there, but You keep it from taking over my life. I give You all praise and glory. In Jesus's name. Amen.

Time with Father

As everyone is at lunch, I found myself alone and needing the quiet. I ate, wandered around the church, and ended up in the sanctuary. It's so peaceful in there. I sat on the front pew, played "Give Me Jesus," and just closed my eyes, waiting. I've felt all morning that Father and I would be having a conversation at some point today. He allowed me the time to soak up the stillness, the music and words that played, and that time I just needed to get my mind in a thoughtful way and ready to spend time with Him. Meditation is my "go-to," but today I didn't take that time. Yes, I spent quiet time with Him, but my norm is to listen to soft music and just focus on a scripture. Today wasn't the day for that. Today I was to be in communication with our Lord, our Father in heaven. How often does this happen to you, and when it does, do you take the time? That's what He desires from us—time with Him. Do you make excuses to not spend that time with Him? I'll be honest—sometimes I do, because, you know, I have dishes or laundry to do, I'm too tired, etc. I have an extensive list; I'm sorry to say. However, when we feel that strong connection in knowing He is calling to us, we need to say, "Yes, Father," and spend that time with Him. No more excuses. I'm happy to say that my time with Father was amazing as always. We talked, He talked, and I listened. I love hearing, and in that, I'm reminded that He loves me and I am a child of God—His child—and He is my Father.

> Do your best to present yourself to God as one approved, a worker who has no need to be ashamed, rightly handling the word of truth. 2 Timothy 2:15
>
> Only fear the LORD and serve him faithfully with all your heart. For consider what great things he has done for you. 1 Samuel 12:24
>
> Complete my joy by being of the same mind, having the same love, being in full accord and of one mind. Philippians 2:2

Notes and Reflections

_____

_____

_____

Prayer

Dear Heavenly Father, thank You for the quiet time that I'm able to take from time to time to just spend with You. I thank You for meeting me wherever I'm at, knowing I just need time with my Father. In Jesus's name. Amen.

One Hour

Today during chapel, we were asked the question, "If you knew you only had one hour to live, what would you do? How would you live it?" This question hit me like a ton of bricks. I really don't know what I would do in that moment. Forget about the initial shock of knowing my time has come and the regrets that would inevitably begin to form in my mind. I would hope I would try to think about this instead. God has given me a lifetime of blessings. I've had many ups and downs, and He has seen me through them all. He has cried with me, held me, listened to me, answered my prayers, prepared me for the life of doing His work, and so on. So for you, during that hour, would you simply sit and thank Him for all He has done for you and in you? Would you regret not saying "yes and amen" to His work He has called you to? Would you be in awe of the fact that in one hour, He would call you home and you would be forever in His holy presence? Every day, every hour, every minute, and every second should be lived for Him to do His work and to know in that last hour that you did everything unto Him. I know that no one likes to think about dying and how much time do we have, but it's inevitable. He knows when our time is up, so shouldn't we live each day not in regret but in His presence? Doing His work? Thanking Him? Praising Him?

> Whatever you do, work heartily, as for the Lord and not for men.
> Colossians 3:23, ESV

Notes and Reflections

_____

_____

_____

Prayer

Dear Heavenly Father, I pray that I remember to live each hour as my last and that, in doing so, what I am doing would bring You honor and glory. Thank You for all You have given me, for Your grace, mercy, and forgiveness. I pray that I may not live my life regretting what I haven't done but praising You for all I've been able to do in Your name. In Jesus's name. Amen.

Broken

I asked myself a question yesterday, and yes, I even answered myself. Do you think God allows us to be broken so He can mend us in a way that will bring Him honor and glory? The answer to myself was "yes." I think that in our lives, we get to that point where we just feel defeated/broken. He is there for us and wants to mend us. He uses peace, love, and understanding and is so very patient. When we are going through life and we feel like we can't face what's coming or the struggle is real, then we need to take that brokenness before Him and allow Him to begin the process. Once we understand that everything is from Him, then our lives will begin to take shape. I've had a few God moments this past week, and while it's taken me awhile to get it, I know that this chapter of my life isn't over; but it will only continue to get better in Him, and today wasn't just the beginning of a new day but a continuation of my journey. Begin your journey with Christ if you haven't yet. Allow Him to lead you, and He will show you the unbelievable.

> Come to me, all who labor and are heavy laden, and I will give you rest. Take my yoke upon you, and learn from me, for I am gentle and lowly in heart, and you will find rest for your souls. For my yoke is easy, and my burden is light. Matthew 11:28–30, ESV
>
> For I know the plans I have for you, declares the Lord, plans for welfare and not for evil, to give you a future and a hope. Jeremiah 29:11, ESV

Notes and Reflections

_____

_____

_____

Prayer

Dear Heavenly Father, I know in my brokenness, You will show me how it can be mended. I pray that in my life, You show me what I need to see, what I need to hear, and the courage to continue the journey You've set before me. In Jesus's name. Amen.

Living for Christ

I'm learning to deal with a very difficult situation in my life. I'm learning that I don't have to be that person who always tries to make friends with someone who simply and clearly doesn't want to be friends and makes it quite clear. Here's the struggle: I'm not great with people not liking me. I know you're probably thinking, "*Who?* Who doesn't like you?" I know, right? Ha ha ha ha (a little humor). Think about this: How many people didn't accept Christ, or did they like or even love Him? Yet He still loved them. No, I'm not comparing myself or my situation to Christ, but I'm thinking about this: Christ is love. Christ is King. Christ should be the *one* constant in my (your) life, no matter what is going on, and He should be the only one that I (you) should concern myself (yourself) with when it comes to who loves me (you). We mess up daily, but He is quick to forgive and still loves us. He doesn't ignore us and is always there for us. We can only do so much when it comes to people we love, and they don't want anything to do with us but not Christ. When it comes to what we can do for Him, there are so many things. So don't worry about what family member or person doesn't like you because Christ loves you, and that, my friends, is all that matters. Live your life for Him, not them.

> So here's what I want you to do, God helping you: Take your everyday, ordinary life—your sleeping, eating, going-to-work, and walking-around life—and place it before God as an offering. Embracing what God does for you is the best thing you can do for him. Don't become so well-adjusted to your culture that you fit into it without even thinking. Instead, fix your attention on God. You'll be changed from the inside out. Readily recognize what he wants from you, and quickly respond to it. Unlike the culture around you, always dragging you down to its level of immaturity, God brings the best out of you, develops well-formed maturity in you. Romans 12:2, The Message [MSG]

Notes and Reflections

_____

_____

_____

Prayer

Dear Heavenly Father, with each difficult situation that I face, I pray, Lord, that I'm able to continue to find my strength in You and know that You are still God in every situation. I pray that I continue to live my life for You and do the things that You would have me to do. In Jesus's name. Amen.

Our Father's Name

I've been thinking lately about my relationship with Christ. It's been lukewarm, and I don't care for that. So this is something I'm working on, and my first step in this journey is how to address our Father in heaven when I begin to pray or when I just feel like speaking with Him. It has taken me a little while because I wanted to address Him as my Father, but I also needed it to be more intimate, and you're probably thinking, "How could it be more intimate?" Well, I asked myself that same question, but I can tell you, for me, I was lacking that relationship of intimacy with Him. So after a great deal of reading, hoping I wasn't doing something wrong by doing this, looking at the meanings of all the different names for Him, and prayer, I chose a way to address Him that just makes that connection with Him even stronger for me. Last night I spoke to Him, and I felt an immediate connection. I felt like I should have been addressing Him this way all along. So now you're probably wondering what name I chose, but I'm not going to tell you because you see, this is *your* relationship with Him, and how you address Him has to be your choice and what brings you closer to Him. There are many, and they each have such an amazing definition. Pastor Monroe Bailey has preached on the different names and their meaning. So if you chose to change how you address our Father, I encourage you to read about the names, but more importantly, pray about it. He will let you know if it's right. Trust me, but more importantly, trust Him.

Notes and Reflections

_____

_____

_____

Prayer
Dear Heavenly Father, I pray that I continue to speak to You, but more importantly, I begin to listen. I thank You for accepting the way I address You in my prayers and the connection that has brought to us. Thank You for allowing me to know that I can trust You and, in that trust, what is right is shown to me. In Jesus's name. Amen.

The Word: Part 1

Over the weekend, something was said to me that really made me stop and think. It was said, "One day people will be hungry for the Word of God and the teachings because it will be illegal and people will have to hide. It may not happen in my lifetime, but it's coming." And all I could think was, "Wow!" Right now we live in a country where we (as families) are able to attend worship on Sunday without worrying about being persecuted, we are able to worship on Wednesday (adults and kids programs), and really, we are able to worship 24-7 without fear. So I guess with the above statement, I have to wonder, Why aren't we hungry for the Word of God now? Why can't we give Him our undivided attention for more than a couple of hours a week when we know that He is giving us 24-7? He gives us His time whenever we need Him and even when we don't think we need Him. He's still there. Shouldn't we want to hear more and more about Christ and be taught all we can soak up? I know I want that. When you pray tonight, thank Him for being in a country that He is allowed and there's no hiding. Be in the Word because right now we're allowed to read the Word of God in the open. Be in constant prayer and time with Him. There is no hiding.

> And he said to all, "If anyone would come after me, let him deny himself and take up his cross daily and follow me. Luke 9:23, ESV

Notes and Reflections

_____

_____

_____

Prayer
Dear Heavenly Father, I pray for those who have to hide because they believe in You. I lift each and every Bible study that takes place, that they not be found out, and that each time they meet, their faith continues to grow. I pray that they remain hungry for your Word and that You continue to watch over them. In Jesus's name. Amen.

The Word: Part 2

I wanted to follow up on our reading of the Word and being able to worship without having to hide. We all know that in other countries, having to hide is a fact. They are so hungry for the Word of God that they risk their lives to worship and learn about Him in secret, hoping no one tells and they are found out. We live in a free country, and yet our reading of His Word is really taken for granted. But think about something. What would you do if tomorrow that freedom was suddenly taken away? What would you do if our Bibles were confiscated? Would you be able to bring forth what you have read? We need to be in the Word daily, even several times a day, a verse or two. We need to be reading our Bible and storing those words in case we don't have actual books someday. It's a scary thought, isn't it? So we need to be hungry enough for the Word of God to learn it, live it, teach it, and preach it. Soak it all up all you can, and ask Him to help you.

> But the Advocate, the Holy Spirit, whom the Father will send in my name, will teach you all things and will remind you of everything I have said to you. John 14:26, NIV
>
> Heaven and earth will pass away, but my words will not pass away. Matthew 24:35, ESV

Notes and Reflections

_____

_____

_____

Prayer
Dear Heavenly Father, thank You that I live in a country that doesn't consider being a Christian, going to church, and going to Bible study to be a crime. I thank You that I am able to carry my Bible with me daily. I pray that the fire continue to burn for me to have that desire to read Your Word, to talk to others about Your Word, and to live it out. In Jesus's name. Amen.

One Day

I've been reminded quite a bit lately that I need to make changes in my life and that the first change I need to make is putting Father first. He needs to be my priority—not second, third, or fourth. I used to never think about it, and when I had time for Him, then I had time for Him. That's wrong on so many levels because, you see, He doesn't just "make time" for me but He has made me a priority as He has you. He doesn't think, "Well, I guess since I haven't spent much time with Joan, I should probably do that." No, He makes every day a Joan day, a Kim day, a Linda day, a Barb day, a Beth day, an Anita day, a Pastor Monroe Bailey day, and so on with everyone. Sometimes it's difficult to make that time and make the changes that we need to make. However, He's waiting. He's waiting for us to make the changes in our lives that allow us to spend time with Him and to live the life He has for us to live. Think about this: What if, one day, He no longer made us a priority because we didn't make those changes nor did we make Him our priority? I know I would be devastated, and I know I would have no one to blame but myself. Thankfully, He doesn't work that way. Again, He makes us a priority and wants to see those changes in us. Take the time. Make the changes. You won't be sorry. He loves you.

> But seek first the kingdom of God and his righteousness, and all these things will be added to you. Matthew 6:33
> So whether we are at home or away, we make it our aim to please him. 2 Corinthians 5:9
> You shall love the LORD your God with all your heart and with all your soul and with all your might. Deuteronomy 6:5

Notes and Reflections

_____

_____

_____

Prayer

Dear Heavenly Father, making changes has never been easy for me, so I lift up the changes to You and the decision to spend time with You in place of other things in my life. I pray, Lord, that I make every day a day spent in thoughtful prayer and scriptural meditation. Go with me through each chapter that changes, and allow me to know that You are priority. In Jesus's name. Amen.

Your Attention

This morning, I was told there are three hurricanes, two earthquakes, and the wildfires going on at this time. So as I'm writing this morning, my heart and prayers go out to all who are in the midst of the many storms going on. I've heard several people say, "Wake up, people. God is trying to get your attention." I used to say that as well, but I've since learned otherwise. So here's my response to that: Why should it take a hurricane, earthquake, or wildfire to get your attention? He should have already gotten your attention when He went to the cross, and shouldn't the Word of God get your attention? Shouldn't learning on Sunday morning or Wednesday nights get your attention? Here's the thing: He wants to have our attention always. It shouldn't be in the midst of the storms that we give Him our attention. It should be all the time. I mean, after all, it doesn't take a disaster in our own lives before He pays attention to us, so why should it be any different? I'm guilty of this, as we all are at different points in our lives. Don't wait until there is a disaster in your life to give Him your full attention. But if you do wait, just know that He's there to help you through it; and while we don't always see it at the time, He steers us away from many disasters. Thank Him, praise Him, and give Him all the Glory during the bad times and the good times.

>Give your entire attention to what God is doing right now, and don't get worked up about what may or may not happen tomorrow. God will help you deal with whatever hard things come up when the time comes. Matthew 6:34

Notes and Reflections

_____

_____

_____

Prayer

Dear Heavenly Father, I pray that I continue to keep my attention on You in the good as well as the bad. I pray that during any time, I continue to praise You and to know that you are in the midst of it all. Be with those who aren't sure, and allow them to see you during those times and during the good times. In Jesus's name. Amen.

Time

You've all heard the saying, "You get out of it what you put into it." Well, that goes for so many things in my life and yours. But when I was thinking about this, my thought was on God. I was thinking about the many blessings, my relationship with Him, and my small part of ministry. I'll be the first to say that even with the Bible-reading plan done at church, I'm behind. In my prayer time, I'm behind. In just simply spending time with Him, I'm behind. So what does that mean in terms of where I'm at with Him, and am I getting everything He wants me to have? Probably not. He never holds back, yet He wants to give me so much more. Where are you with "putting into it" with Him? Like me, do you need to spend more time with Him? Reading? Praying? Be honest, because you see, when we spend our time with Him in all ways possible, He loves that. And in doing so, the blessings He will pour out and the better our days will be as we focus on Him will be more than we could ever imagine. So put 110 percent into spending that time with Him, and watch what comes out of it.

> But seek first his kingdom and his righteousness, and all these things will be given to you as well. Matthew 6:33
>
> He says, "Be still, and know that I am God; I will be exalted among the nations, I will be exalted in the earth." Psalm 46:10

Notes and Reflections

_____

_____

_____

Prayer
Dear Heavenly Father, I pray that I learn to spend more time with You. I pray that my time will be spent in prayer and reading Your Word also. I know that I allow the busyness of this life to interfere in my day and my time, so I ask that You help me to set aside time for You. In Jesus's name. Amen.

Change

Change happens, and my best friend always says, "Change is good." She's right, of course, but I don't do well with change (ask my family/friends). I've always been an "if it ain't broke, don't fix it" kind of person. That is, until I finally allowed God to take over my life a few years ago, and *wow*, did He begin a change in me. You see, like many, I was broken and still am in some ways, but the pieces are slowly coming together. I always thought, "I am who I am, and I'll always be this way." I'm glad I was wrong because I love the changes, and I give Him all praise and glory. I have found my passions, and He has equipped me to handle them and to use them and, I pray, in doing so show others who Christ is and what it means to have a life with Him. When we allow Him to make those changes in us, He smiles. At least, that's how I see it. When we fight against Him, where does that get us? I fought Him too long, but no more. I pray and I listen. I'm where He wants me to be and doing what He has put on my heart to do. Am I finished? Absolutely not. I'm just getting started. My faith walk and my faith growth have gotten stronger, and my journey with Him is amazingly beautiful as well as the changes in me. My encouragement to you is to get onboard and allow the changes to happen because they will be a journey like none other.

> Do not be conformed to this world, but be transformed by the renewal of your mind, that by testing you may discern what is the will of God, what is good and acceptable and perfect. Romans 12:2
>
> For at that time I will change the speech of the peoples to a pure speech, that all of them may call upon the name of the LORD and serve him with one accord. Zephaniah 3:9

Notes and Reflections

_____

_____

_____

Prayer

Dear Heavenly Father, thank You for the changes in my life, and I thank You for fixing the broken pieces that used to be my life. I pray that I may continue to walk in Your strength and continue to grow in You. In Jesus's name. Amen.

The Past

How many take blood pressure medicine? I'm sure many do, and for me, last night I could have used a pill or two. Today has been a tough "pill" to swallow (so to speak) in a review of my attitude, and I'm sorry to say that I allowed the past circumstances and situations to dictate my attitude and how I felt in that moment. Why do we do that? Why do we allow ourselves to give that power to someone else? What we should be doing instead is mindfully praying, praying for a better attitude about someone and praying not only *for* that person but that God can teach us to have a more loving attitude toward them. Lessons hurt sometimes, but the outcome is beautiful. God, thankfully, never dislikes us. He loves us. I'm sure He is, however, from time to time, disappointed in us, but that doesn't mean He stops loving us. I'm thankful for that. And I'm thankful He convicts me because without that conviction of knowing what I think and feel are wrong, what would happen? I can tell you, it wouldn't be good. He gives me the grace, mercy, and forgiveness even though I far from deserve it, and so shouldn't I do the same? Shouldn't I be forgiving and show grace? Don't allow the past to keep you from enjoying the present, and when you feel you're at the end of your wits, give it to God. Feeling His love and peace flow through you far outweighs anything else you have going on.

> A joyful heart is good medicine, but a crushed spirit dries up the bones. Proverbs 17:22
>
> And whatever you do, in word or deed, do everything in the name of the Lord Jesus, giving thanks to God the Father through Him. Colossians 3:17

Notes and Reflections

_____

_____

_____

Prayer

Dear Heavenly Father, I lift up to You my attitude, and I pray that it be more Christlike in every way. Lord, help me to learn from my mistakes and to not continue to make them. I pray that I become more forgiving of others as You have been forgiving of me. In Jesus's name. Amen.

Childlike Faith

This morning at church, I was watching Sheila dance around the church with the littles and the happy look on their faces because in that moment, they only knew that they love Jesus. They are praising Him in a way that makes not only Him happy but them as well. She brings out the giggles and grins in them. They have, as they should, a childlike faith. Where is your praise and worship? Is it so grown-up that you've forgotten that you are, in fact, a child of God? He wants us to praise Him in singing (whether you can carry a tune or not), rejoicing in Him, clapping our hands, raising our hands up to Him, praying with a childlike faith, and just focusing on Him. My praise and worship isn't as "out there" as some, and I've decided that it's okay until a couple of weeks ago. God had other plans. During the closing song, I found myself raising my hand to Him in worship. The song moved me beyond anything I could have imagined. This act of worship was so outside the box for me, but it was a wonderful feeling knowing that it was just Him and I in that moment. So think about how you worship Him. Are you playing it safe? Are you worried about how others will think of you? I used to be, and while it's not my "every Sunday in church" type of worship, I'm glad He allowed me that time. I would like to say that it was *my* time in which I did this, but I know in my heart that it was *Him*.

> Let everything that has breath praise the Lord. Psalm 150:6
> Praise the Lord, my soul; all my inmost being, praise his holy name. Psalm 103:1

Notes and Reflections

_____

_____

_____

Prayer

Dear Heavenly Father, thank You for allowing me to have a childlike faith in You. I pray that Your light shines through me as I am a child of God. I pray that I may continue to be outside the box in my praise and worship that it gives You all praise and glory. In Jesus's name. Amen.

Movies

Today I was able to finally watch *The Shack*. I have the book and have read it a couple of times, but if you haven't had a chance to read it or watch it, please take the time to do so. While I know it isn't based on a true story, the message is based on the true story of how much God loves us and is there for us in every moment and situation of our lives. He wants us to come to Him before we get to that moment of destruction of who we are. He created us to be loved by Him, and isn't it a shame we so often forget this? While watching the movie, I was brought to absolute tears because I saw myself in so many of the situations of the movie. No, I have never lost a child, but I know many of you reading this have, and that part touched my heart in ways that will keep me praying for you and your loved ones because I can't imagine the pain. The movie just brought out everything I know in my heart I've been doing wrong and not allowing God to be a part of in order to heal and change. How many of you can relate to this? We spend our time wanting so much to do what's right, yet instead, we play judge and jury; we don't give to God our hurt and anger over someone doing us wrong, we don't forgive, and so many other things. I spent quite a bit of time in prayer after watching the movie, and I know I'm not finished. But as I am writing this, I feel ashamed that it took a movie for me to be on my knees in prayer and realize all the things I need to get right in my Christian walk. If you're there today, I encourage you to be in close prayer time with God and allow Him to begin your healing process, forgiving process, and anything else that needs His attention. He's waiting.

> If then you have been raised with Christ, seek the things that are above, where Christ is, seated at the right hand of God. Colossians 3:1, ESV
>
> If we confess our sins, he is faithful and just to forgive us our sins and to cleanse us from all unrighteousness. 1 John 1:9, ESV

Notes and Reflections

___

___

___

Prayer

Dear Heavenly Father, thank You for loving me even at my worst and even when my faith in You wavers just a bit. Thank You for never walking away, even though sometimes I do. Thank You for welcoming me back with open arms. In Jesus's name. Amen.

Music

Music takes me to places I wouldn't normally go. Do you ever just get caught up in a song and you immediately go to Him? Sometimes it takes a song to get us focused back on God. I was thinking this afternoon about the sermon and loving God with our all. I was listening to "Keep Your Eyes on Me," and there's a part in the song that when it just gets to that point of knowing, I close my eyes and listen; I can feel the presence of God. In that moment, I close my eyes and I give Him everything I am. Music can be an important part of praise and worship. I will admit that not all songs touch my heart the way some songs do. I can get so caught up in the moments of the words and the melody that I push the world away and focus on Him. It sounds odd, but I love Him through music too. I can sing and talk to Him about loving Him with everything I am. How do *you* spend your time loving Him with your all? Do you have special times or songs you go to when you just want it to be you and Him? If not, find it. He loves when you take more time than just Sunday morning or Wednesday Bible study to spend with Him.

> Give me your heart, my son, And let your eyes delight in my ways. Proverbs 23:26
>
> Then Jesus said to His disciples, "If anyone wishes to come after Me, he must deny himself, and take up his cross and follow Me. Matthew 16:24

Notes and Reflections

_____

_____

_____

Prayer

Dear Heavenly Father, thank You for the music that You bring to my life. I'm thankful that many times, a song will play at just the right time. I thank You that I'm able to find peace and a connection with You through the words being sung. In Jesus's name. Amen.

Victory in Jesus

What do you think about when you hear, "I have victory in Jesus?" Do you think about the obstacles you've overcome because of your faith in Him? Does your mind go to where you used to be and where you are now? I used to hear that and think, "What victory do I have in Jesus?" I had to go outside the box in my thinking on this one because just looking at my life, I wouldn't just come up with anything. Yes, I have gone beyond where I ever thought I would be at this time in my life, but I could hear myself saying, "Victories?" So in my thinking, yes, I have many many victories in Christ Jesus. Let me share one with you that I wouldn't have considered to be one but, really, it is: understanding a scripture you've read many times and you finally got it (victory!). It may seem like "really?" But *yes*! But my greatest victory is in knowing Who my God is and knowing His Son, Jesus Christ. Whenever we accomplish something or even have that moment of clarity, those are victories in Jesus. We can have small victories, or they can be huge. Either way, they count. Think outside the box today, and begin to think about yours. They're there. Just look, and in each one, remember Whom to give all praise and glory.

> But thanks be to God, who gives us the victory through our Lord Jesus Christ. 1 Corinthians 15:57
>
> But thanks be to God, who always leads us in triumph in Christ, and manifests through us the sweet aroma of the knowledge of Him in every place. 2 Corinthians 2:14

Notes and Reflections

_____

_____

_____

Prayer

Dear Heavenly Father, I thank You for the victories, no matter how small that I have in You. Lord, I pray that each and every day, I learn more of You and remember to give You all praise and glory. In Jesus's name. Amen.

Battles

Have you heard the phrase "You have to pick your battles"? I thought about that today as I fight with my inner self on different issues. There's one issue that I've decided has to be a battle I choose not to fight. The end result won't be any better than the beginning, so why fight it? Right? Well, what if God thought that way about us? What if He said, "Why pick this battle I won't win and the end result won't be any better than the beginning?" The good news is that He doesn't say that or even think it. He loves us and believes we are worth fighting for, and He does so every day. He even knows the outcome. If you think back or even think about a present battle you are facing or battles you have faced, did you face them alone? Absolutely not. He was there all the time. He was and is fighting *for* you, *not* against you. We struggle in life because in the midst of the battles, we wonder if He is there. But ask yourself this: Did you seek Him out to help you? Did you pray about it and ask Him to equip you for battle? Allow Him to take up your fight. Give Him your battle. I promise you that His beginning was and His end will be greater than you could imagine.

> The Lord will fight for you, and you shall hold your peace. Exodus 14:14
>
> You will not have to fight this battle. Take up your positions; stand firm and see the deliverance the LORD will give you, Judah and Jerusalem. Do not be afraid; do not be discouraged. Go out to face them tomorrow, and the LORD will be with you. 2 Chronicles 20:17, NIV
>
> The Lord will march out like a champion, like a warrior he will stir up his zeal; with a shout he will raise the battle cry and will triumph over his enemies. Isaiah 42:13, NIV

Notes and Reflections

_____

_____

_____

Prayer

Dear Heavenly Father, thank You for fighting for me through the battles in life. I pray that I am able to learn to just give them to You in knowing that You've got them. Thank You for loving me so much that in the end, the battle of life will be won and You will be victory in You. In Jesus's name. Amen.

The End of the Day

I was thinking about the "end of the day." How is it that every evening before going to sleep, my mind goes in a million different directions and I worry and wonder about my day? Did I do enough? Did I do something to help someone? Was I kind? Did I make a difference? My thought list goes on and on, but I think one thing that really stands out for is this: Did I forgive, not only others but myself as well? While everything else is important, that for me is at the top of my list. I know that more often than I'd like to admit, I didn't forgive (at least in that moment, sometimes it takes me a few days as I'm a tad on the stubborn side). So then I think, "Well then, why would I think that I should be forgiven?" So at the end of the day, at the end of *your* day, where do you stand on forgiveness? Have you forgiven, not only someone, but have you forgiven yourself? What if, at the end of the day, Christ decided not to forgive us for what we had done because it was pretty bad and we didn't appear to be sorry and He decided to be stubborn? How unsettling is that thought? I don't know about you, but I'm so very thankful we serve a loving, forgiving, and grace- and mercy-giving God. So what I'm saying is this: Don't wait to forgive someone. And don't wait to forgive yourself.

> For if you forgive other people when they sin against you, your heavenly Father will also forgive you. But if you do not forgive others their sins, your Father will not forgive your sins. Matthew 6:14–15

Notes and Reflections

_____

_____

_____

Prayer
Dear Heavenly Father, please help me to remember that You forgave me and I should forgive others. I pray that at the end of the day, I've shown Who You are through my words and actions. Thank You for being over my life and teaching me every day the way I should be to others. In Jesus's name. Amen.

God's Timing

Yesterday at our staff meeting, the question was asked: What has God written on your heart that's important? I've really thought about that because I know what He has written on mine, and I pray I don't let Him down in trying to do things in a way that will bring Him honor and glory. He has written things on our heart because more often than not, it's something that you've thought about and is a passion but have maybe pushed it aside. In so many ways, He gives us the tools we'll need to make that passion come to life. It's exciting when we see what He wants to use us for and in a field you may have forgotten about. My desire to do mission work came at such an early age that I really did push it aside until last year. He has been preparing me all along so when *His* time was right, I would be ready. That's what He does, and what an amazing God we serve. I have a couple of other things that I had felt He has written on my heart, and each day I get to work on them with Him. I never leave Him out of my day and especially when it comes to doing His work. If you're feeling that God has written something on your heart, I encourage you to pray about it and pray for clarity. He'll show you how to begin, what to do, and the tools you'll need to make it grow and how to continue. Trust Him.

> Whatever you do, work at it with all your heart, as working for the Lord, not for human masters. Colossians 3:23
>
> "For I know the plans I have for you," declares the Lord, "plans to prosper you and not to harm you, plans to give you hope and a future." Jeremiah 29:11

Notes and Reflections

___

___

___

Prayer

Dear Heavenly Father, I want to believe that Your timing is so much better than my wanting things right now. Lord, I ask that in Your timing, I learn where You would have me do Your work. I pray that my trust in You continues to grow and that I know You have work for me to do in Your name. In Jesus's name. Amen.

Talking to the Lord

Yesterday I posted on my Facebook page: "It doesn't matter how old I get. Talking to my momma makes everything better." While that's true, I've been thinking this morning that I shouldn't have just limited myself to just talking to my mom. I should have included talking to the Lord because, really, shouldn't we? Shouldn't we take everything to Him? I'm not saying don't talk to your mom or whomever it is you talk to about life stuff, not at all. But I think we do this because we get an answer right then, even if we don't like it. This goes back to wanting a microwave answer from God when, like Pastor Monroe Bailey says, we serve a Crock-Pot God. Everything is answered and done in *His* time, not in the time cook of 1.75 (popcorn time) that *we* want or a twenty-second microwave muffin (no, I don't cook; yes, I microwave a lot). I talk to my mom a lot about almost everything, but I should also be taking it before the Lord because no matter how wonderful we feel the answers are that we get from someone else, His are always better, much better. And yes, we may have to wait for the right answer, but that's just it. It'll be the right answer, and He truly fixes everything. Take your everyday life issues to Him because He already knows what you're struggling with, and watch how it cooks to the end result of perfection in Him.

> Do not be anxious about anything, but in every situation, by prayer and petition, with thanksgiving, present your requests to God. Philippians 4:6

Notes and Reflections

___

___

___

Prayer

Dear Heavenly Father, in this world today, I know how impatient I can be; but, Lord, You are the all-knowing. Lord, I pray that I am able to remember that Your timing is better than my desire to have it right now. I pray for teaching in waiting and not being discouraged. In Jesus's name. Amen.

Foundation

Sometimes in life, at least in my life, our foundation in Christ can get cracks in it. Some are quite large, but others are just small. But either way, they're still cracks and need repaired. How do we do that? We've accepted Christ, and then it began building our foundation. The hope is that your foundation is built with the sturdiest of materials made from being in the Word of God, prayer, attending church, etc., and not sand. When we build our Christ's foundation with sand, it will erode and fall away with the first sign of bad weather. A foundation built with sturdy material can withstand even the harshest of weather we go through. However, with that being said, sometimes the weather we go through can chip away at our sturdy foundation because there are those little areas that are weak. How do we build a stronger foundation in those areas? Yes, you're right. We give them to the Lord. We pray about them; we read His word; and when doing so, He can rebuild our foundation as long as we trust in Him and give Him those weak areas of our lives. I know my foundation gets stronger with each day, but there are still those areas that have chipped away part of it. I'm learning to give Him those areas of my life so that my foundation in Him will be stronger than ever. So what material will you build your foundation on?

> Therefore everyone who hears these words of mine and puts them into practice is like a wise man who built his house on the rock. The rain came down, the streams rose, and the winds blew and beat against that house; yet it did not fall, because it had its foundation on the rock. But everyone who hears these words of mine and does not put them into practice is like a foolish man who built his house on sand. The rain came down, the streams rose, and the winds blew and beat against that house, and it fell with a great crash. Matthew 7:24–27, NIV

Notes and Reflections

_____

_____

_____

Prayer

Dear Heavenly Father, I know sometimes my life is a bit on the shaky side of the foundation. I pray that, with You, I am able to build stronger the foundation of my faith. I pray that You are with me each day and teaching me how to build it up in You. In Jesus's name. Amen.

Sweeter Side of Life

There are so many sayings for living a better life than the one you are living. For example, there is a sweeter side of life, or the grass is always greener on the other side, just to name a couple. What makes you think that things are better somewhere else? It's funny because I always thought that if I could just, (   ) then I'd be happy. I used to think that things would be better if I lived somewhere else or was working at a different place, things of that nature. But the truth is, I got tired of searching, and my life, being on this side of the fence, is pretty sweet. I, first and foremost, have a Father that loves me more than anyone else could; I work at a church (nothing else to add there); I get to serve the Lord in so many ways, which are ways I never could have imagined; and I have family and friends that love me. So I don't feel a need to keep searching for that "sweeter life" or "greener side." I'm truly blessed, and I know I'm where I am supposed to be in my life. I've come to accept many things (with the help of our Lord), and I'm finally at a place in my life where I know I'm going to be okay. Find that peace within your heart, and know that it's God. We can have such a sweet life in Him, and we truly don't have to search very far. He's always closer than you think.

> For we are his workmanship, created in Christ Jesus for good works, which God prepared beforehand, that we should walk in them. Ephesians 2:10
>
> Therefore, if anyone is in Christ, he is a new creation. The old has passed away; behold, the new has come. 2 Corinthians 5:17

Notes and Reflections

_____

_____

_____

Prayer

Dear Heavenly Father, thank You for my life and that I'm learning to be happy with who I am and, more importantly, who I am in You. You know that I've searched for so long and I did so without You. I thank You that I'm learning to search with You, and I thank You for allowing me to see You in every aspect of my life and knowing it's all good. In Jesus's name. Amen.

Conversation

This morning's devotion really opened my eyes to my way of conversing with others and with God. It talked about complaining (yes, be honest; we all do this) and instead of doing that, to talk to God and allow Him to put His thoughts in your mind. As soon as I read it, this last week came to mind. I'd made an appointment back in July, and it has changed on me five times. So I made a couple of calls, and I was able to get an appointment in a place that God knew was the right place for me. But instead of *just* thanking God (although I did), I had to throw in my complaint about the other. Now, I'm sitting here thinking, "Did that really bring God *all* the glory?" Instead of complaining about the other, I should have been one-hundred-percent giving Him all praise and glory and thanking Him for stepping in. While I'm still thinking about this, my weight feels lighter, and I know God is in this. He is an amazing God, and if we just allow ourselves to hold back on the complaining and the negativity that we speak to others and talk to Him instead, think about everything He can do and will do in our lives. So today, the training begins with an awesome teacher for a better attitude, a heart in doing things without complaint, and more positive words. I pray I find myself talking to Him more and more but not with complaint but with a grateful heart. Sign up for the class. It's free. We should all be taking it.

> Do all things without grumbling or questioning. Philippians 2:14
> Give thanks in all circumstances; for this is the will of God in Christ Jesus for you. 1 Thessalonians 5:18

Notes and Reflections

Prayer

Dear Heavenly Father, I pray that You continue to teach me how to talk to others. I know that I need to begin to see the positive in life and in expressing my words. Thank You for this lesson, and I pray I continue to grow in this way. In Jesus's name. Amen.

God's Timing

Today started out as a run on from last night. It was time (God's time) for me to deal with some things from my past. Now, while I felt like it wasn't something I ever wanted to address, in my heart, I knew God was right. So this morning, I began praying. I prayed for the right words at the right time, I prayed for a peaceful heart, and I prayed that there would be an understanding. My faith in God has really been forefront in my life, especially in the past few months. My talk went great, and I remembered that God had prepared the way as He brought me to this day. He was present and gave me peace during the time I needed Him, and He has been with me since I got home. It's such an amazing thing, isn't it? God's timing? When we don't want to face things or we're waiting on an answer to prayer, it's always His timing. And with the waiting, the end result was more and better than I could have ever hoped for, and I give Him all praise and glory.

>Wait for the Lord; be strong, and let your heart take courage; wait for the Lord! Psalm 27:14, ESV
>
>Be strong and courageous. Do not fear or be in dread of them, for it is the Lord your God who goes with you. He will not leave you or forsake you. Deuteronomy 31:6, ESV

Notes and Reflections

_____

_____

_____

Prayer

Dear Heavenly Father, sometimes I worry about my past showing its ugly head and things that I had hoped to take to my grave coming out. I'm thankful that this one issue is out now and that you were in the midst of my conversation. I thank You that he was understanding, and I pray that he continue to love me. I know, Lord, that this was Your timing and it was a day that was meant to happen. Thank You for the positive outcome. In Jesus's name. Amen.

Our Final Destination

This morning I learned that a family friend has gone home to be with our Lord. She had beat cancer twice, but this time it was her heart. While I've been thinking about her passing this morning, I'm reminded of faith in our Lord. She had such a strong faith. I prayed this morning for her and her family, and I prayed that she had a peaceful passing. I've thought about the faith in which we have in knowing that our life isn't over when we leave this earth but that it's just the beginning with our Father in heaven. It's hard to explain, but it's so huge that I have difficulty wrapping my mind around it. We are here for a time to do the work of our Father that brings Him glory and honor, and the faith we have in knowing that we are heaven-bound is just amazing. Sometimes, I allow it to make me anxious, and it shouldn't because I know my destination. I know that in the end, heaven awaits. So I guess if I have to say anything about our time here, it is that we should always remember that we are here to serve Him and will one day be joined together with Him, and that, my friend, is worth dying for.

> For God so loved the world that he gave his one and only Son, that whoever believes in him shall not perish but have eternal life. John 3:16

Notes and Reflections

_____

_____

_____

Prayer

Dear Heavenly Father, it's never easy when we lose a loved one, but You make it so we are able to get through the situation in knowing our loved one is now with You. Lord, I thank You for being with the families that have lost a loved one, and for me, knowing that I'll be with You at the end of my time here is a comfort and brings me peace. I lift the families up to You that don't know for sure, and, Lord, I ask that You give them strength and peace. In Jesus's name. Amen.

I pray that you got out of this book what God would have you to know in having faith.

He is an amazing God, and each and every day we have life lessons and blessings.

Be a blessing to someone today. God bless.

More to come . . .
Strong and Courageous: Daily Thoughts
The Journey Will Continue

About the Author

J. K. Russell, mother of two and grandmother of four, was born, raised, and still resides in a small Illinois town. She has always enjoyed writing and has had an interest in sharing her walk with the Lord. She is the deacon of missions and has been on two small mission trips with two more planned for the upcoming year. While being involved in the church, part of her ministry includes the Daily Thought she created on the church's Facebook page and is the basis for her book. Her hope is that others will see how God can turn our messes into something beautiful and for His glory. She hopes to continue her writing and sharing the love of God.

CPSIA information can be obtained
at www.ICGtesting.com
Printed in the USA
FSHW012223130819
60979FS